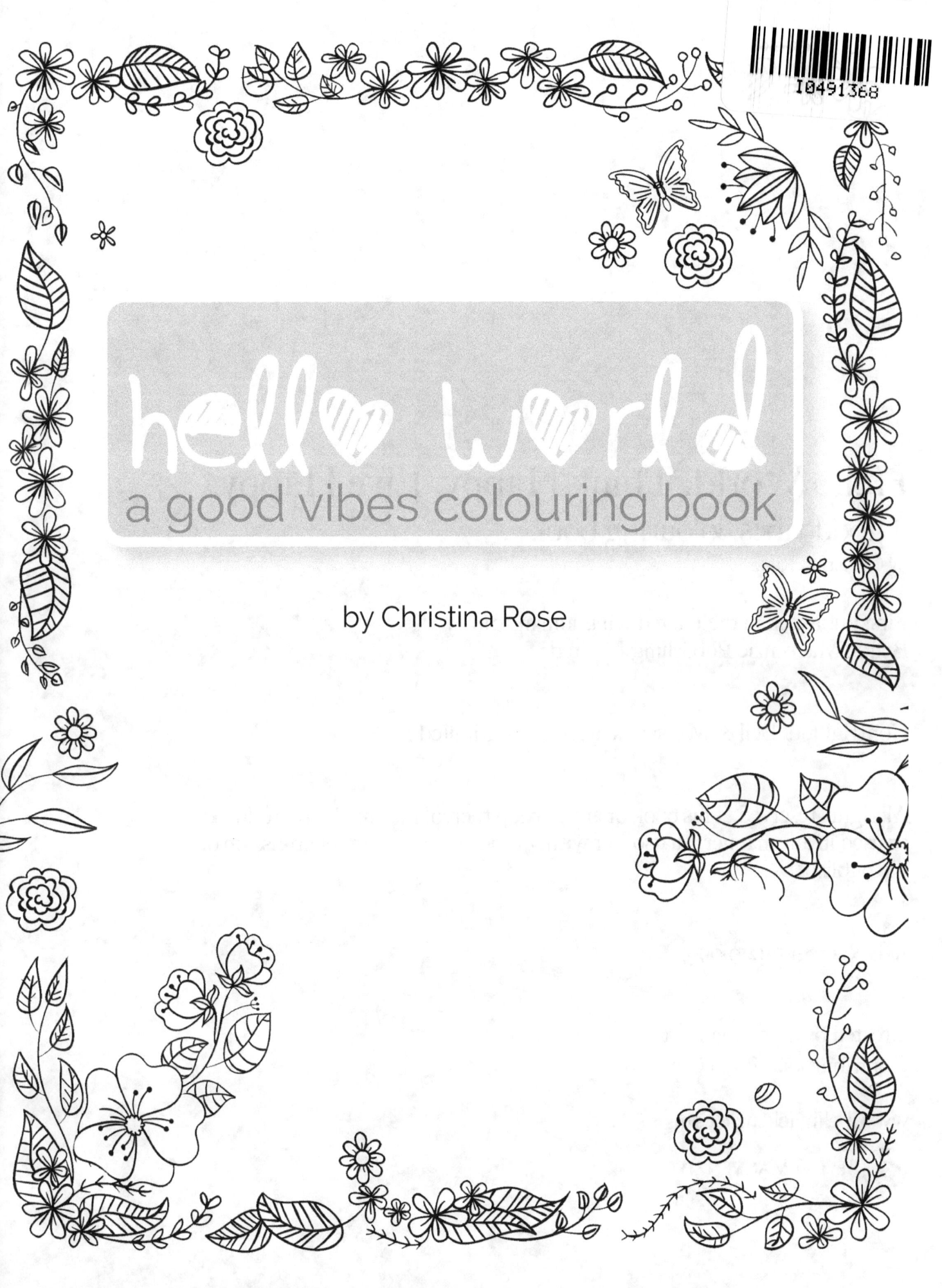

hello world
a good vibes colouring book

by Christina Rose

Hello World: Think Happy. Live Happy.
a good vibes colouring book
by Christina Rose

First published in the United Kingdom in 2016 by
Bell & Mackenzie Publishing Limited

ISBN: 978-1-911219-09-5

Created by Christina Rose
Contributors: Letitia Clouden

www.bellmackenzie.com

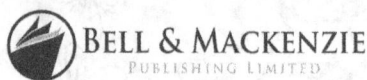 BELL & MACKENZIE
PUBLISHING LIMITED

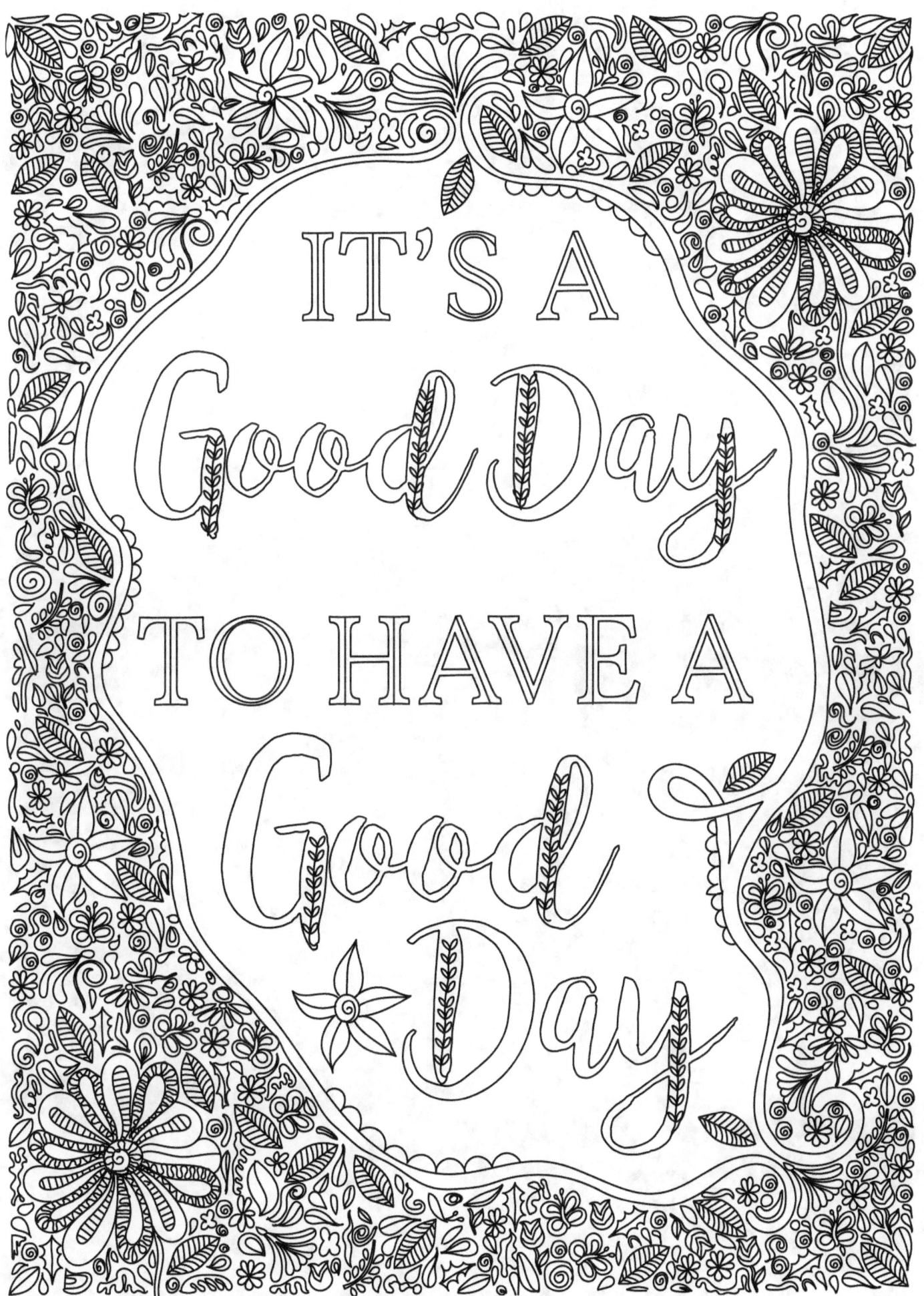

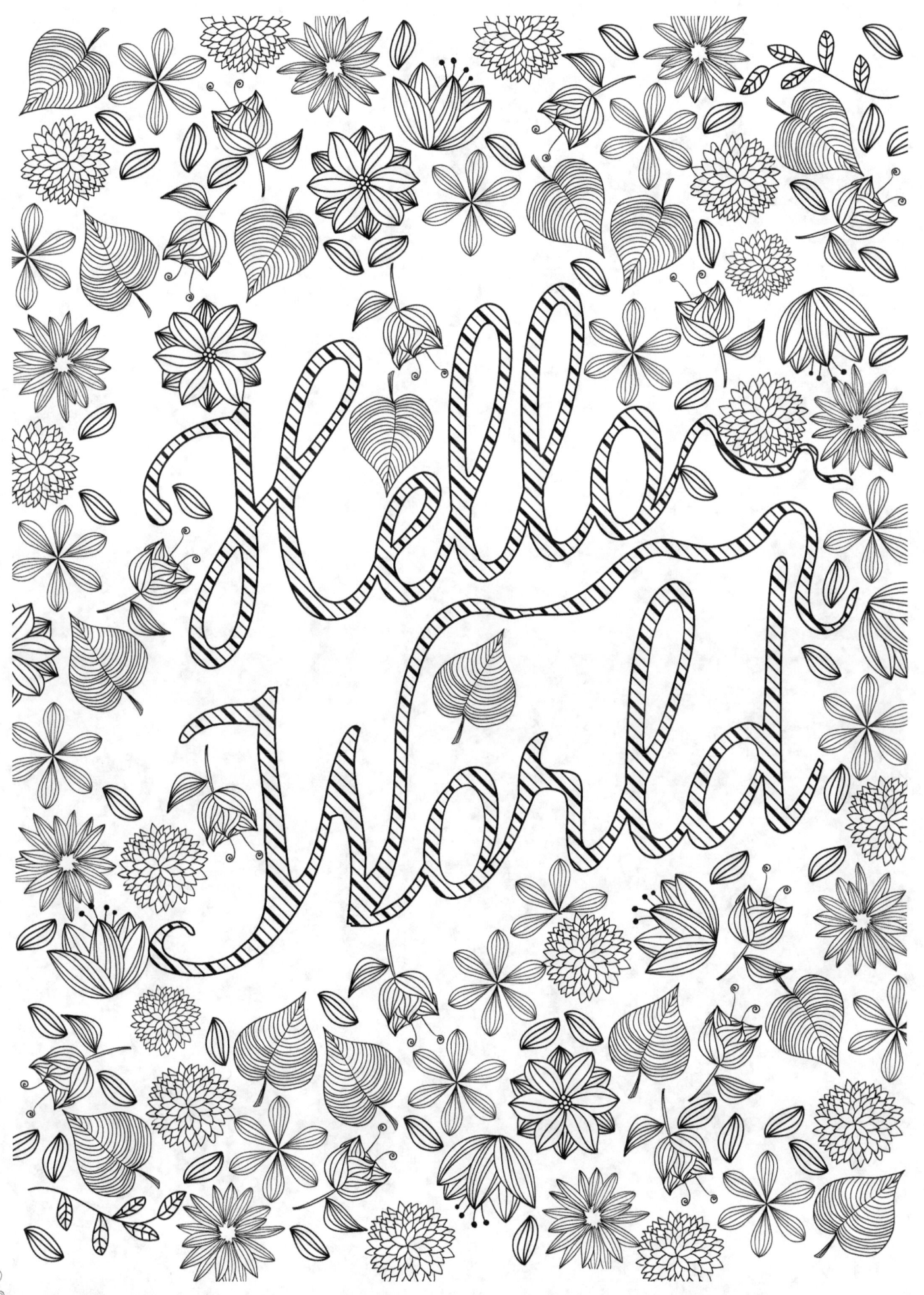

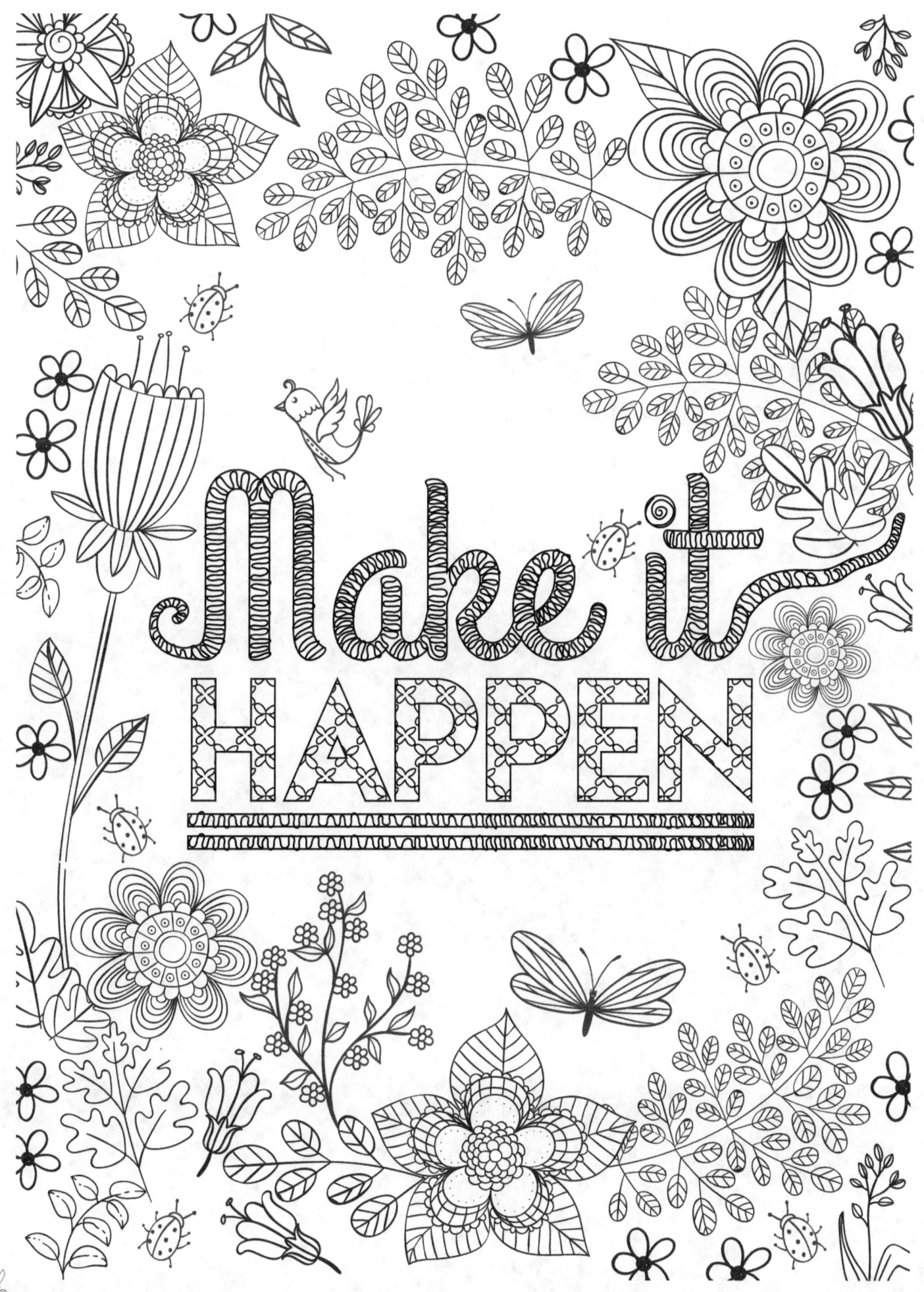

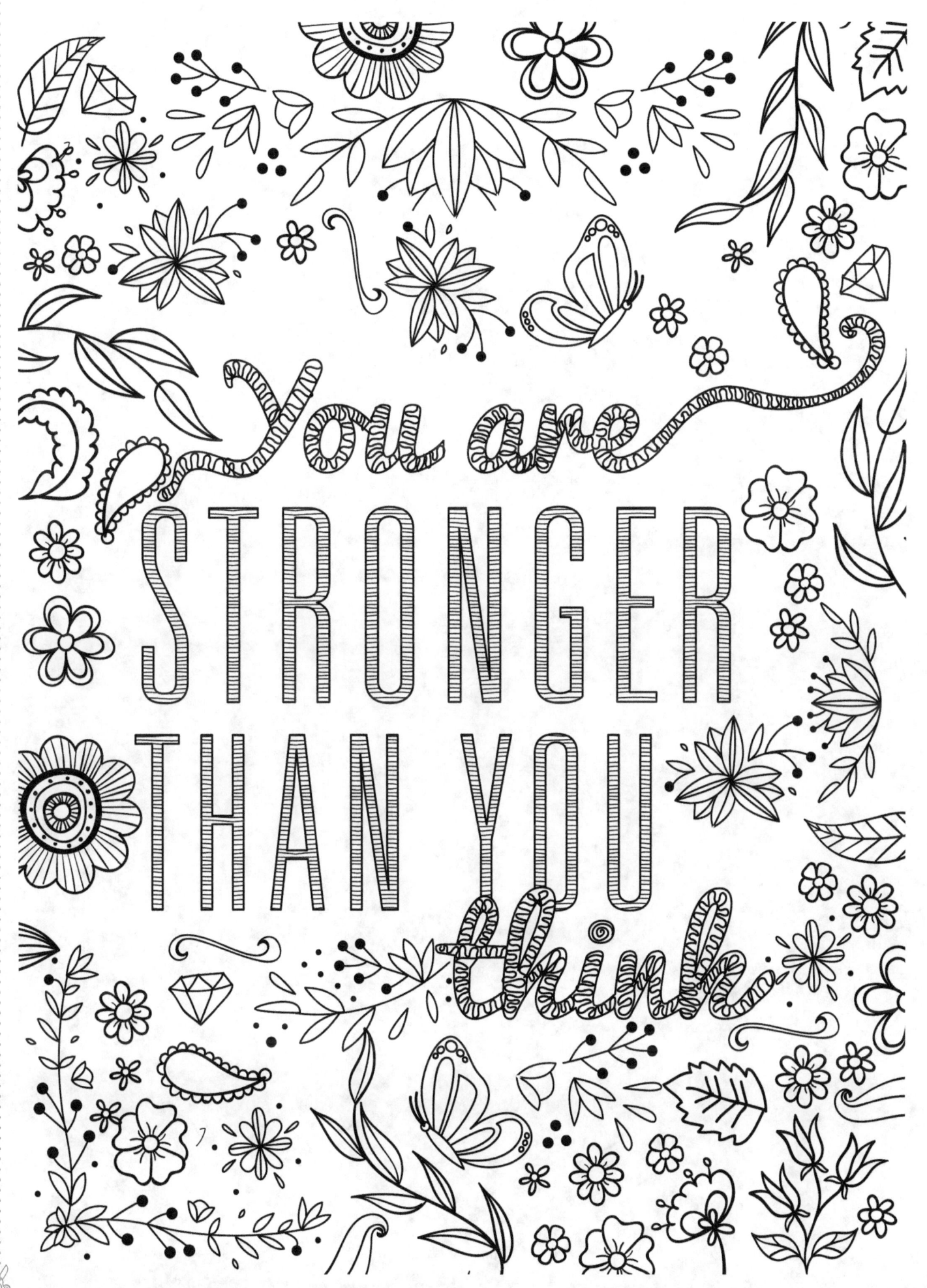

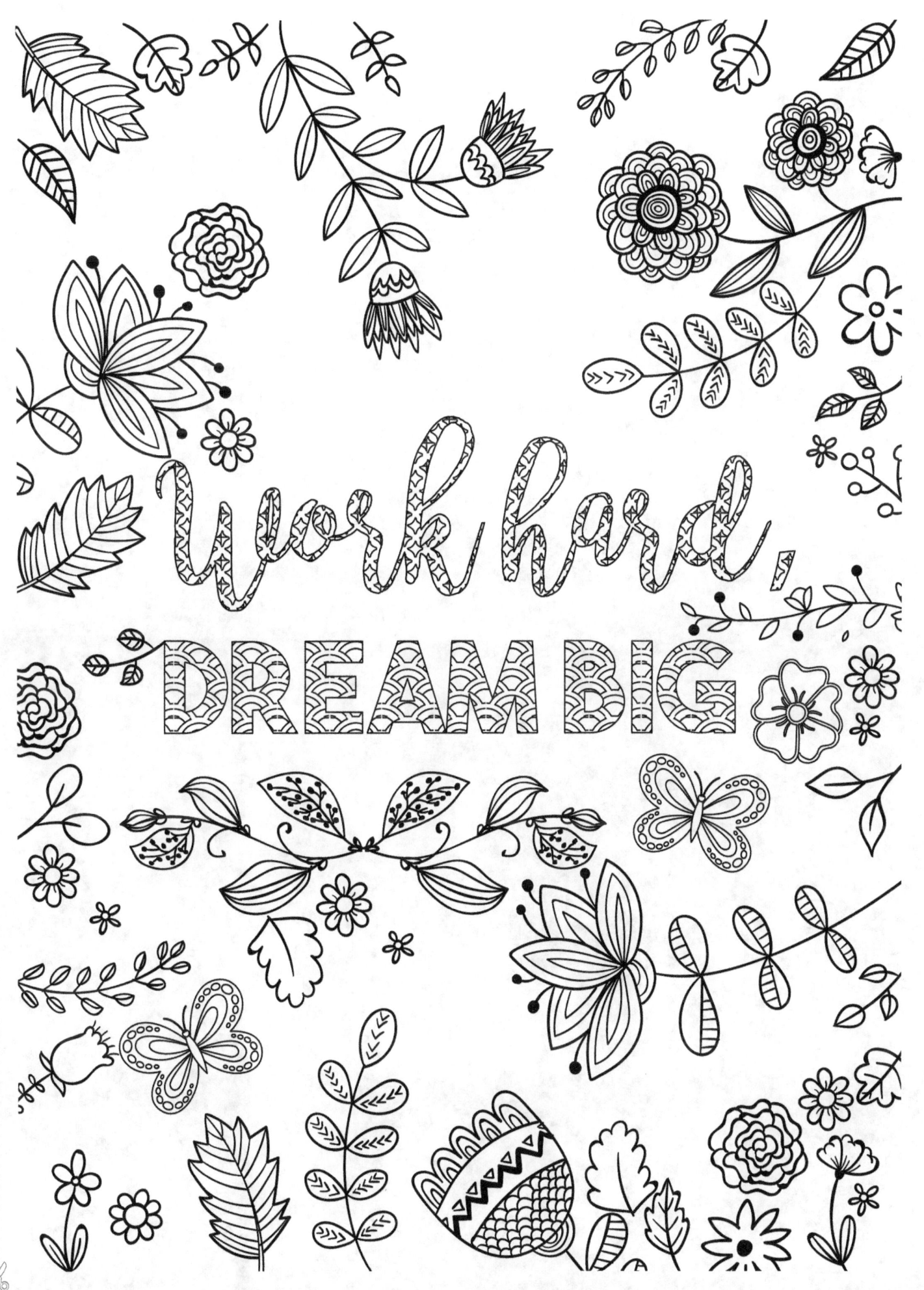

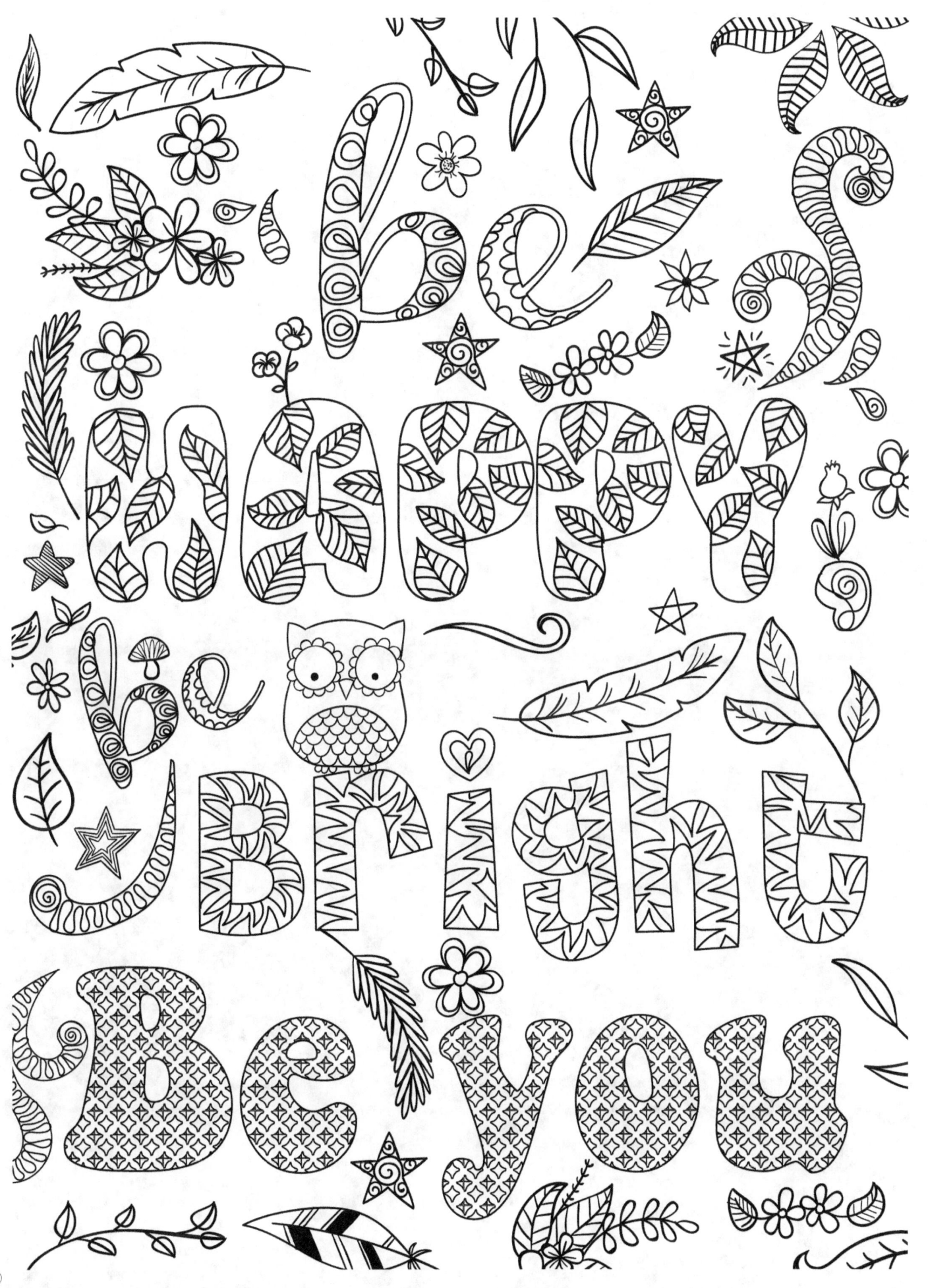

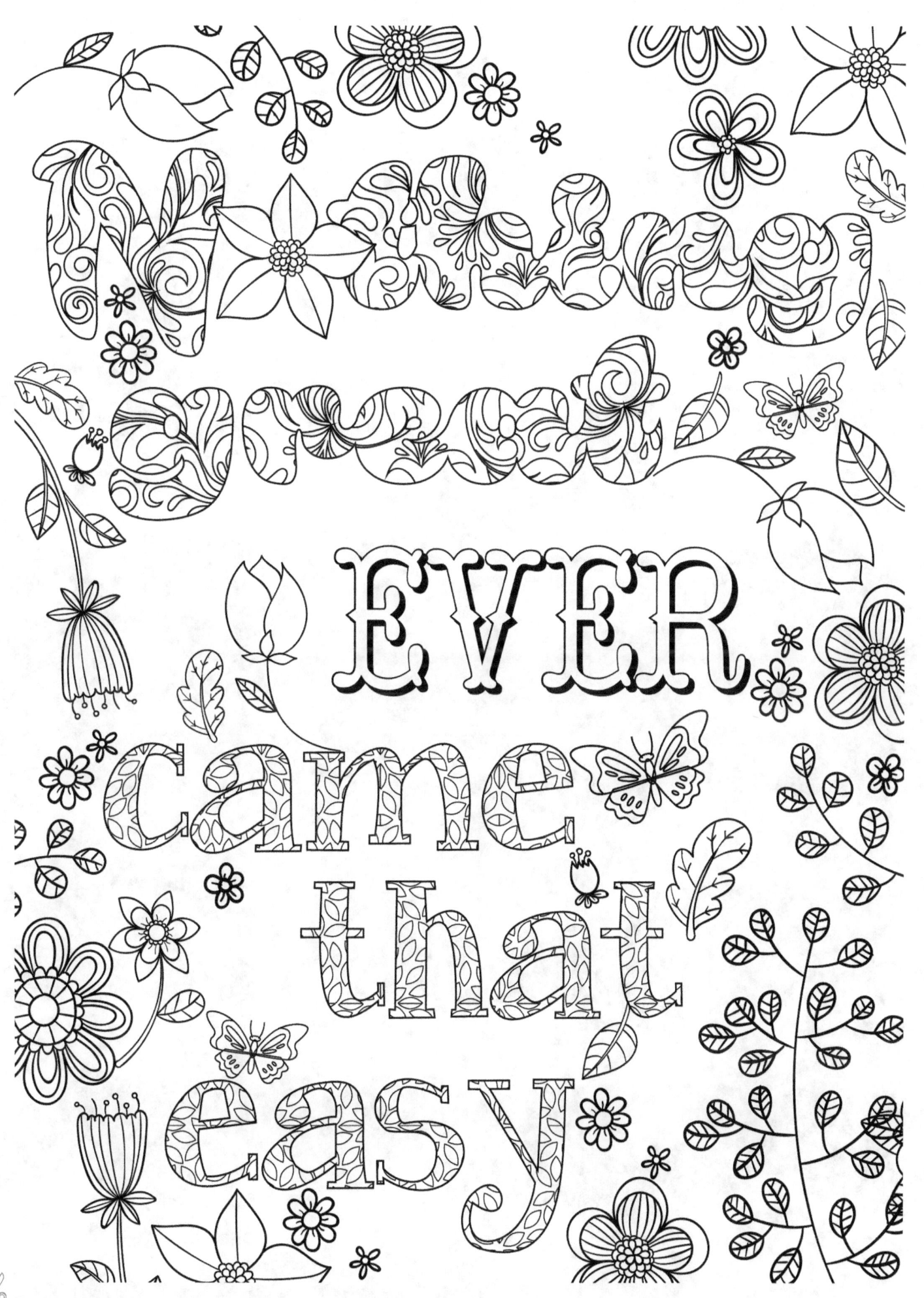

Nothing great EVER came that easy

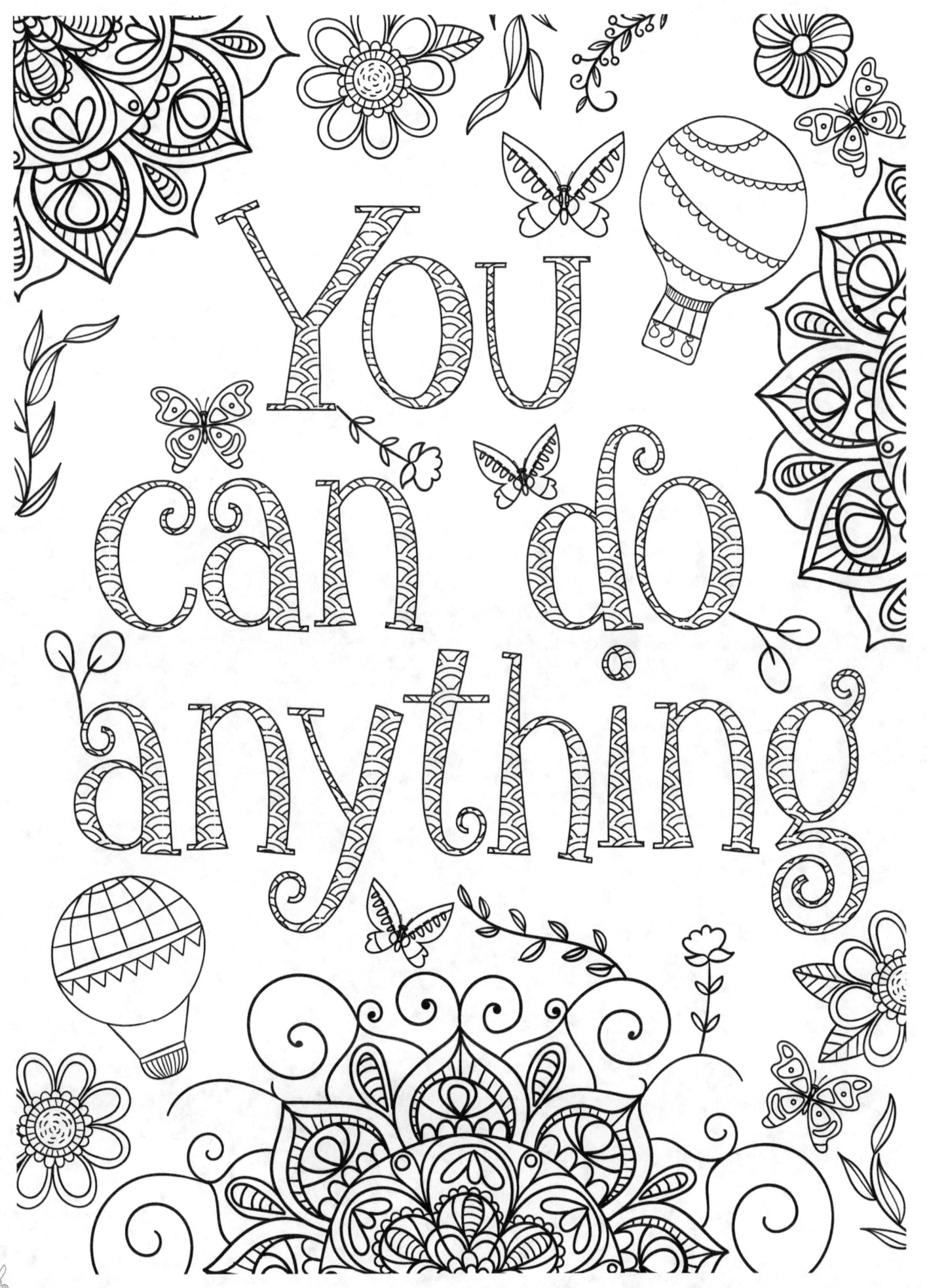

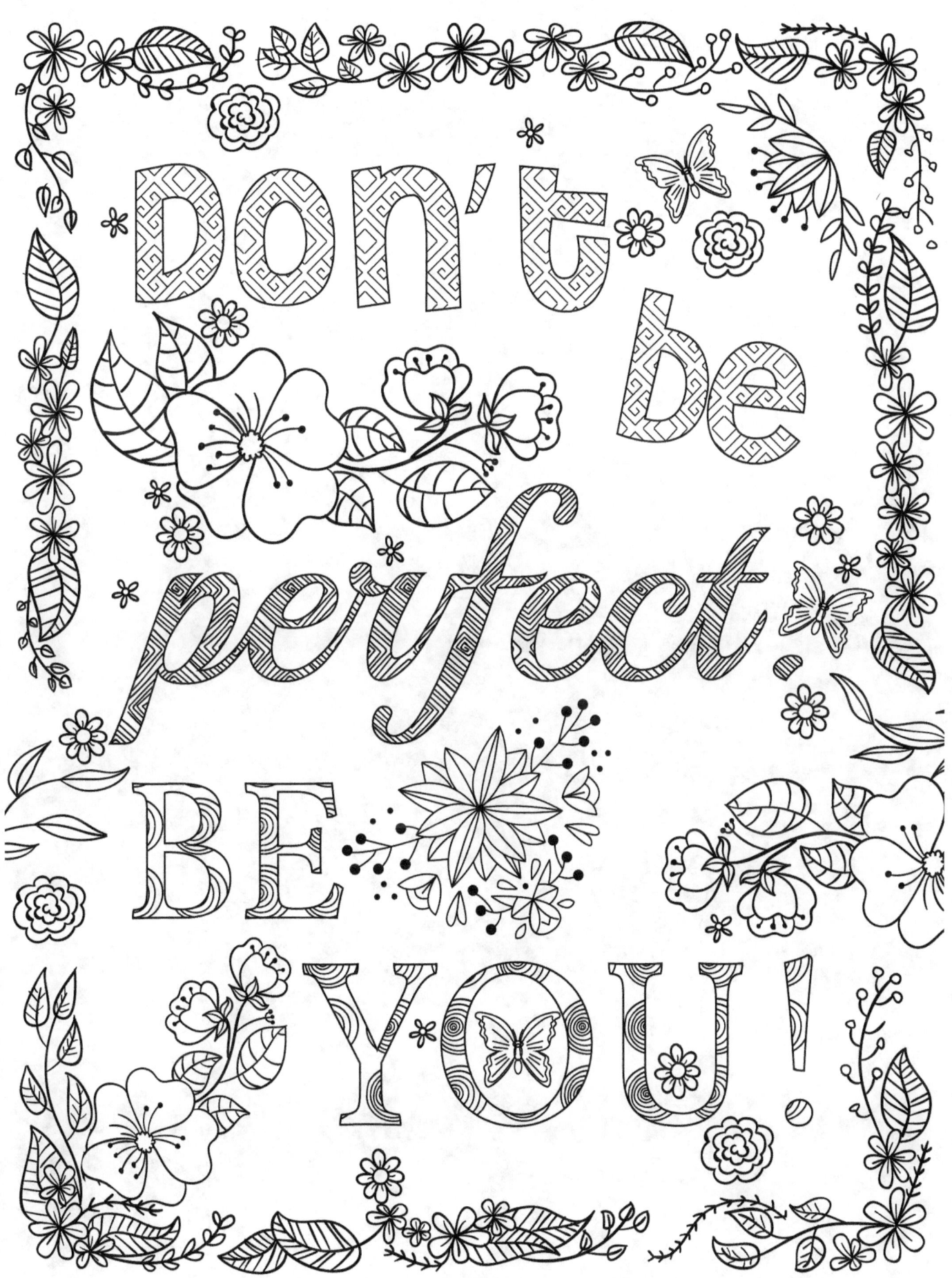

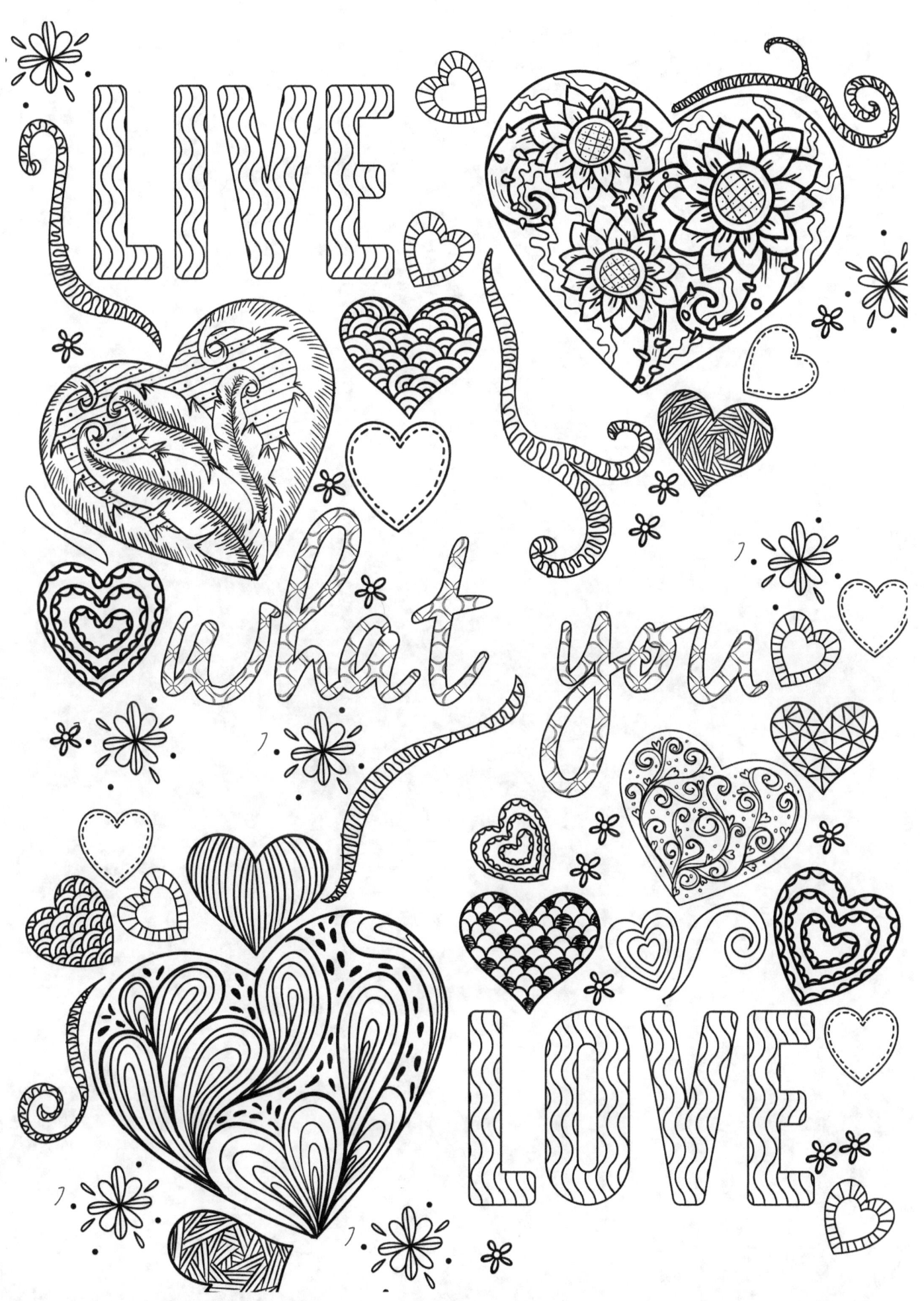

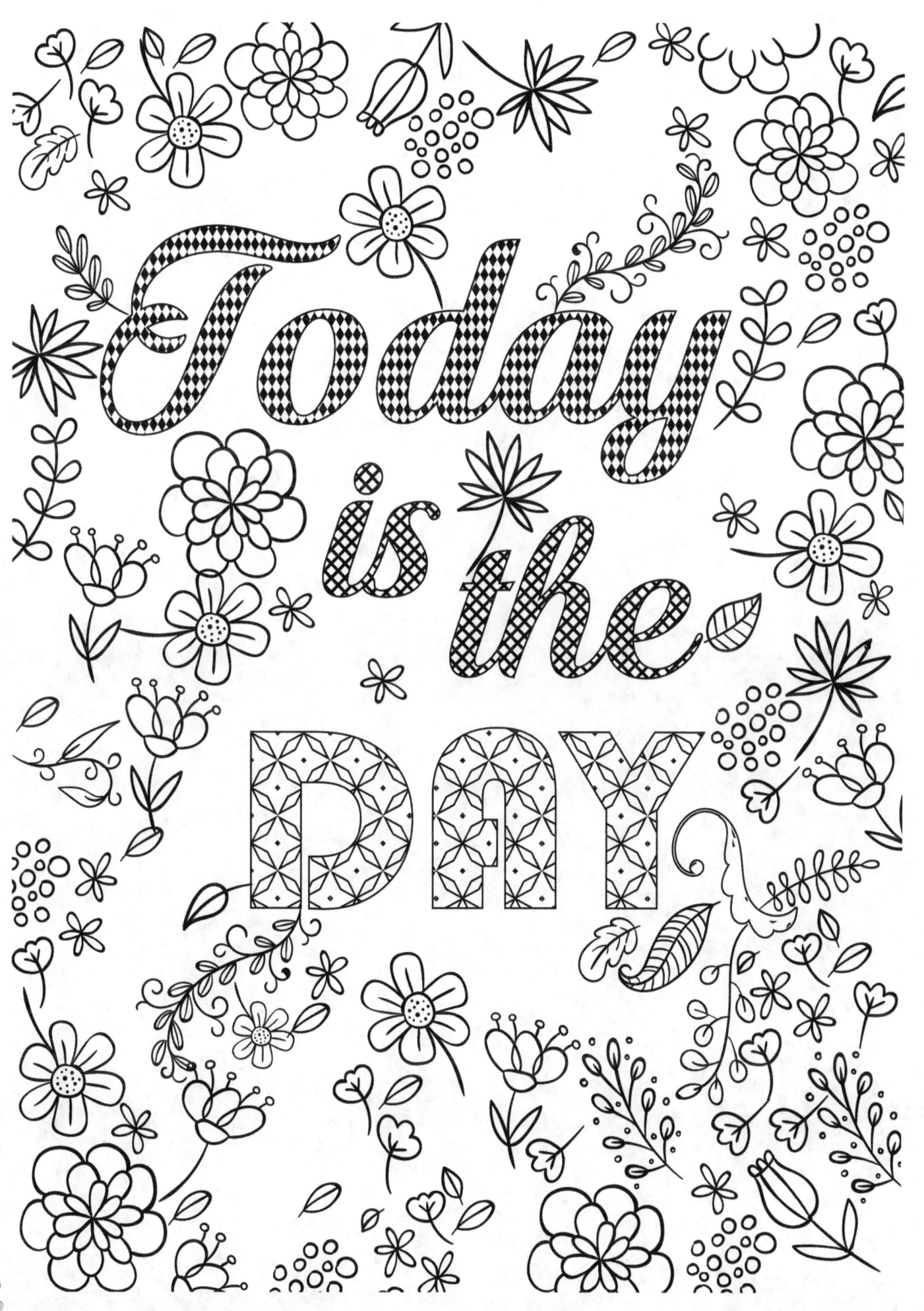

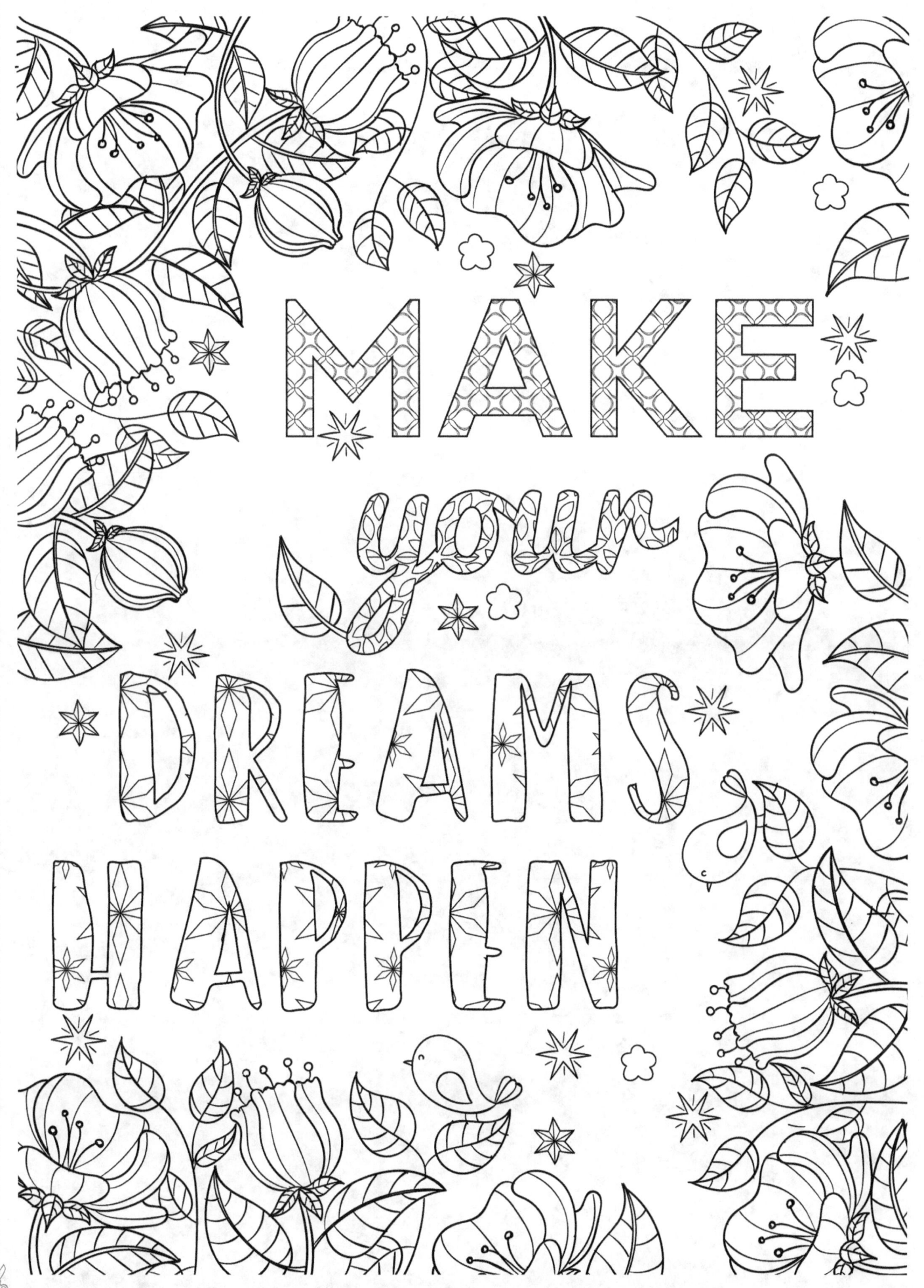

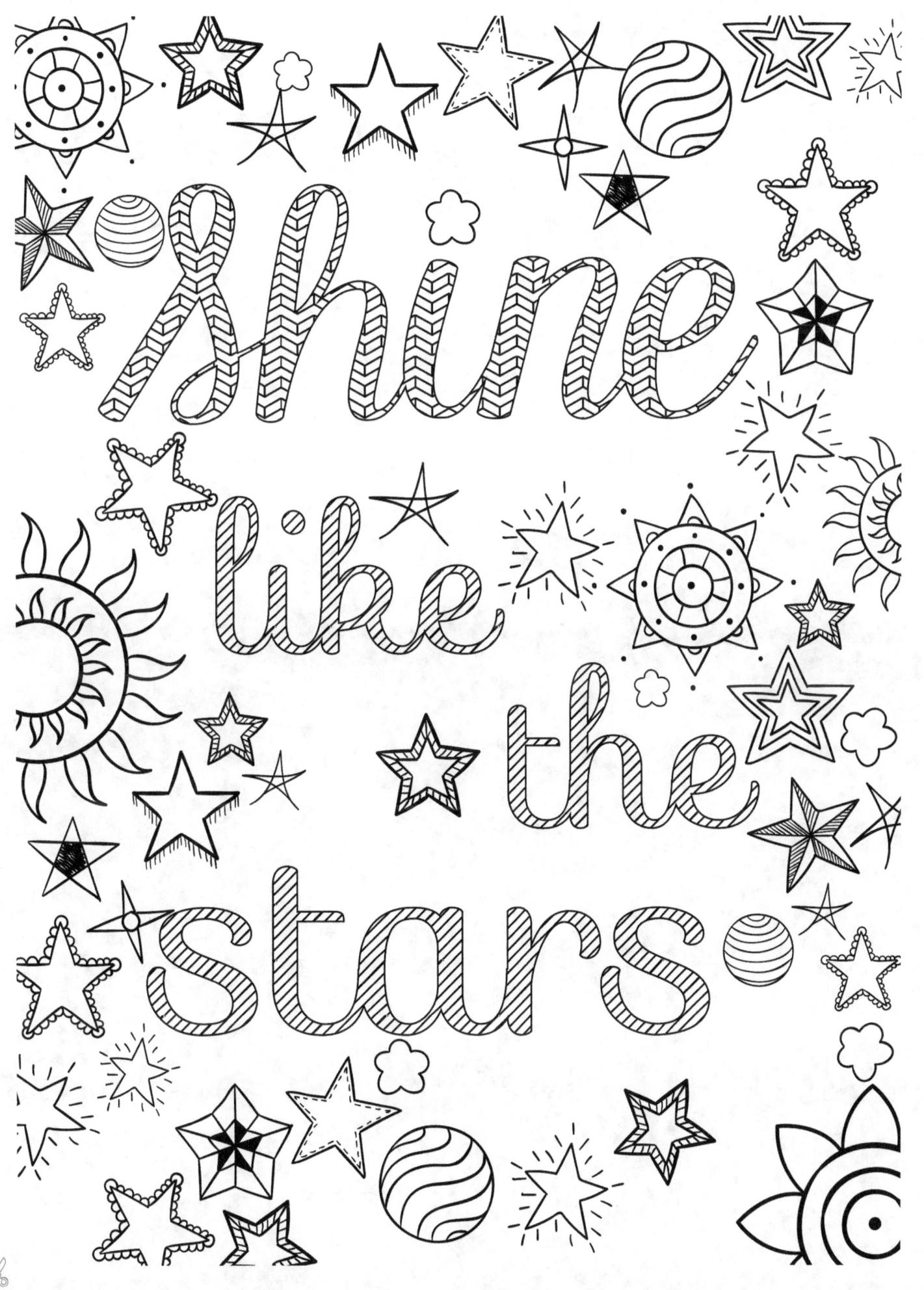

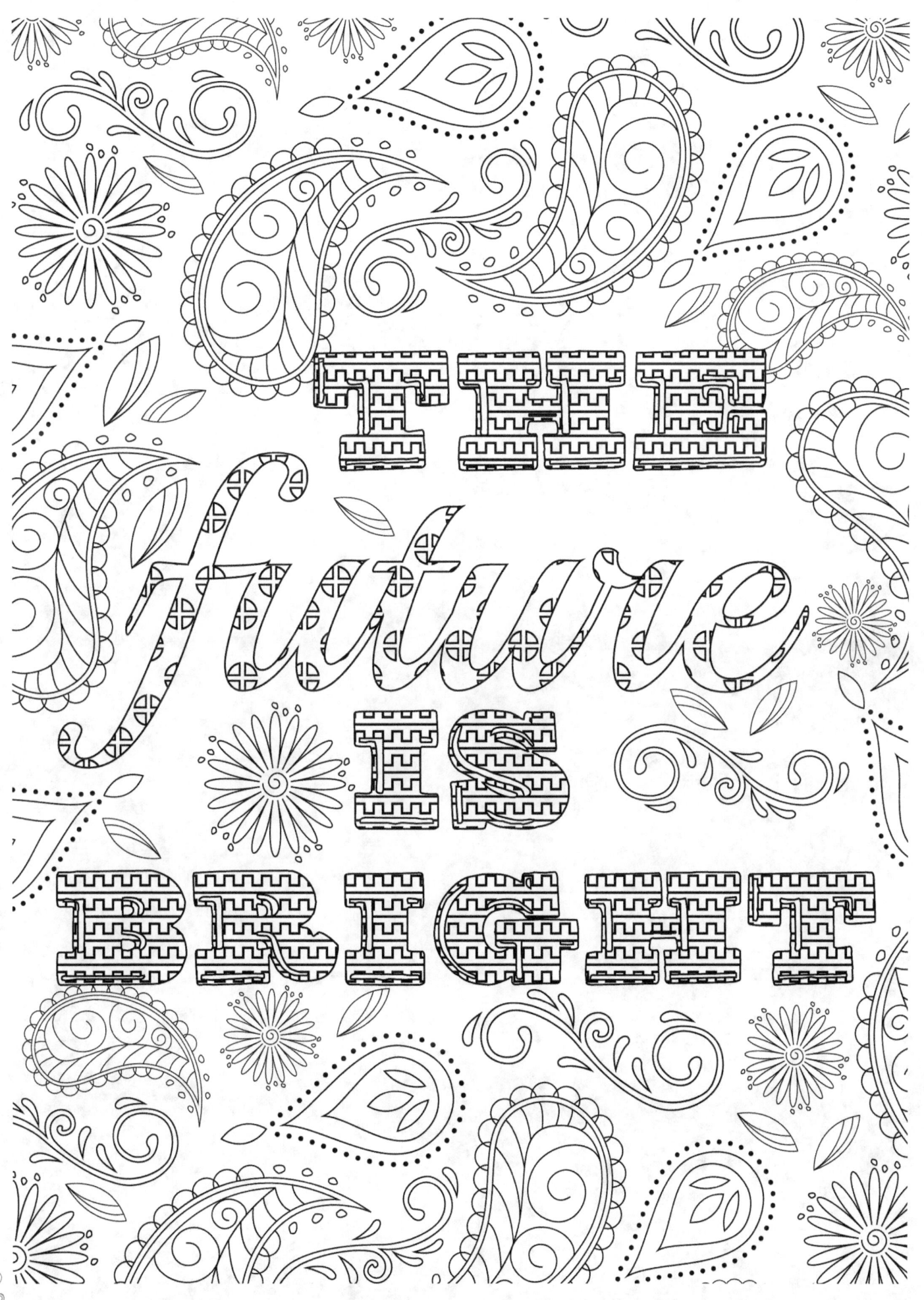

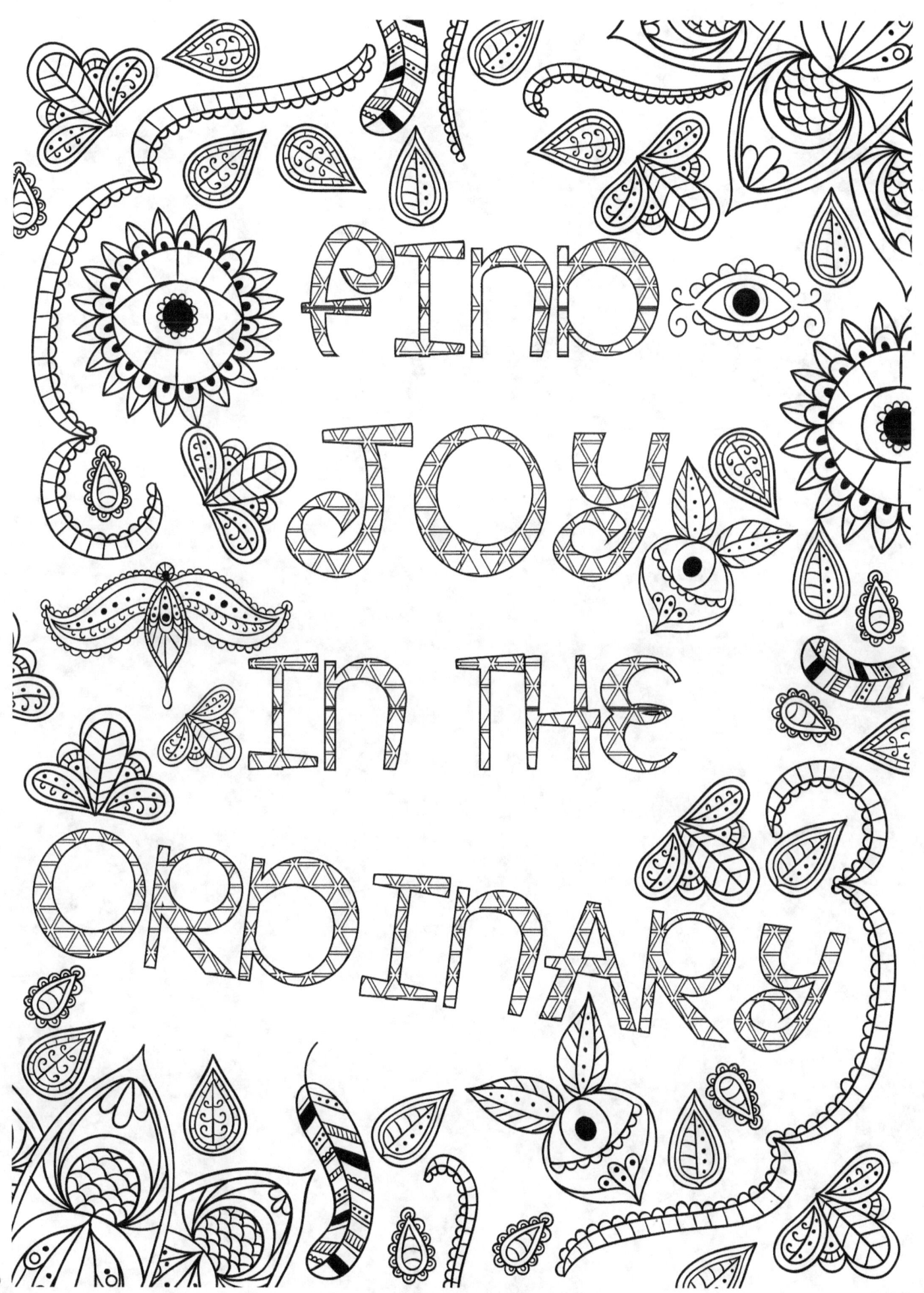

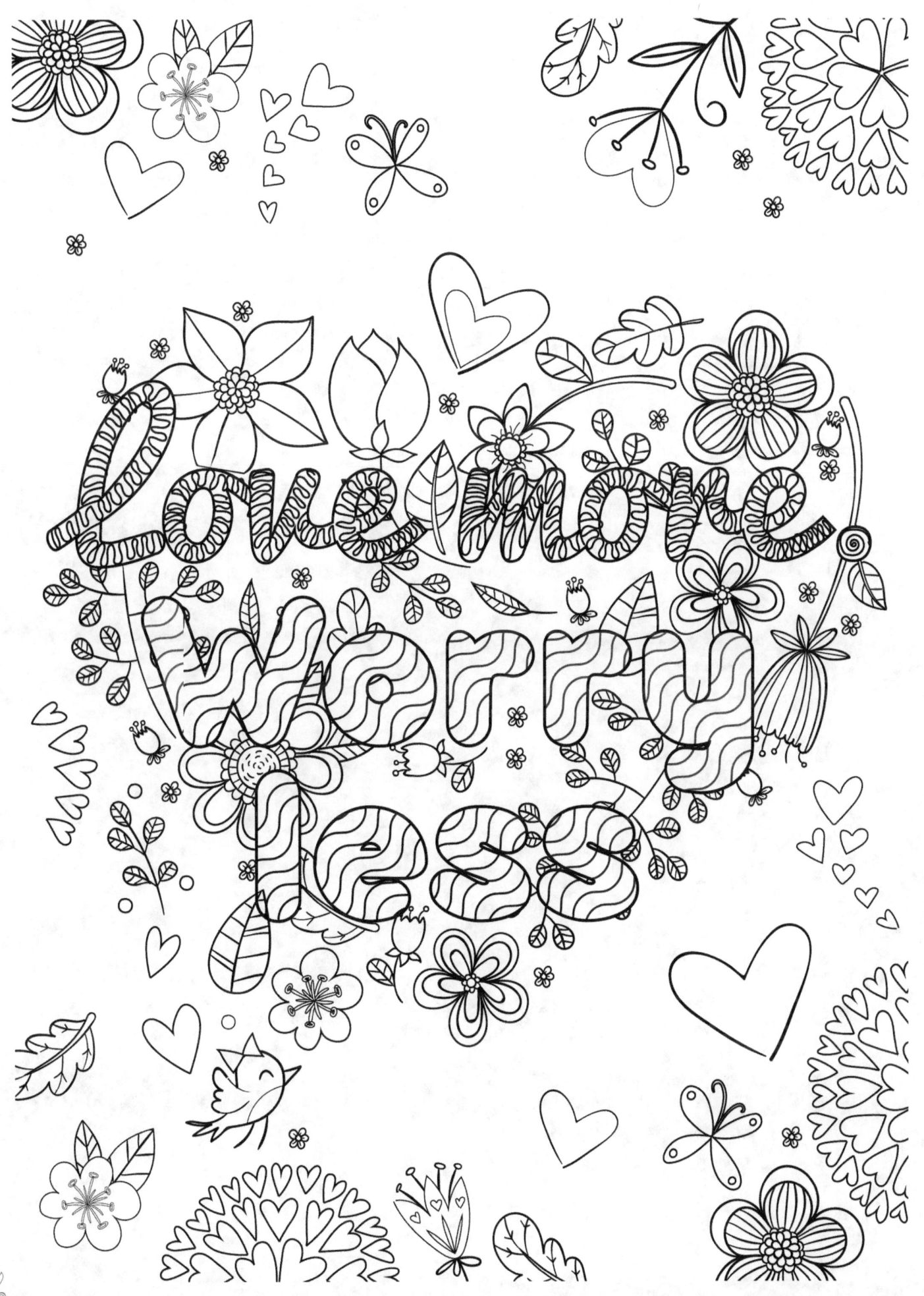

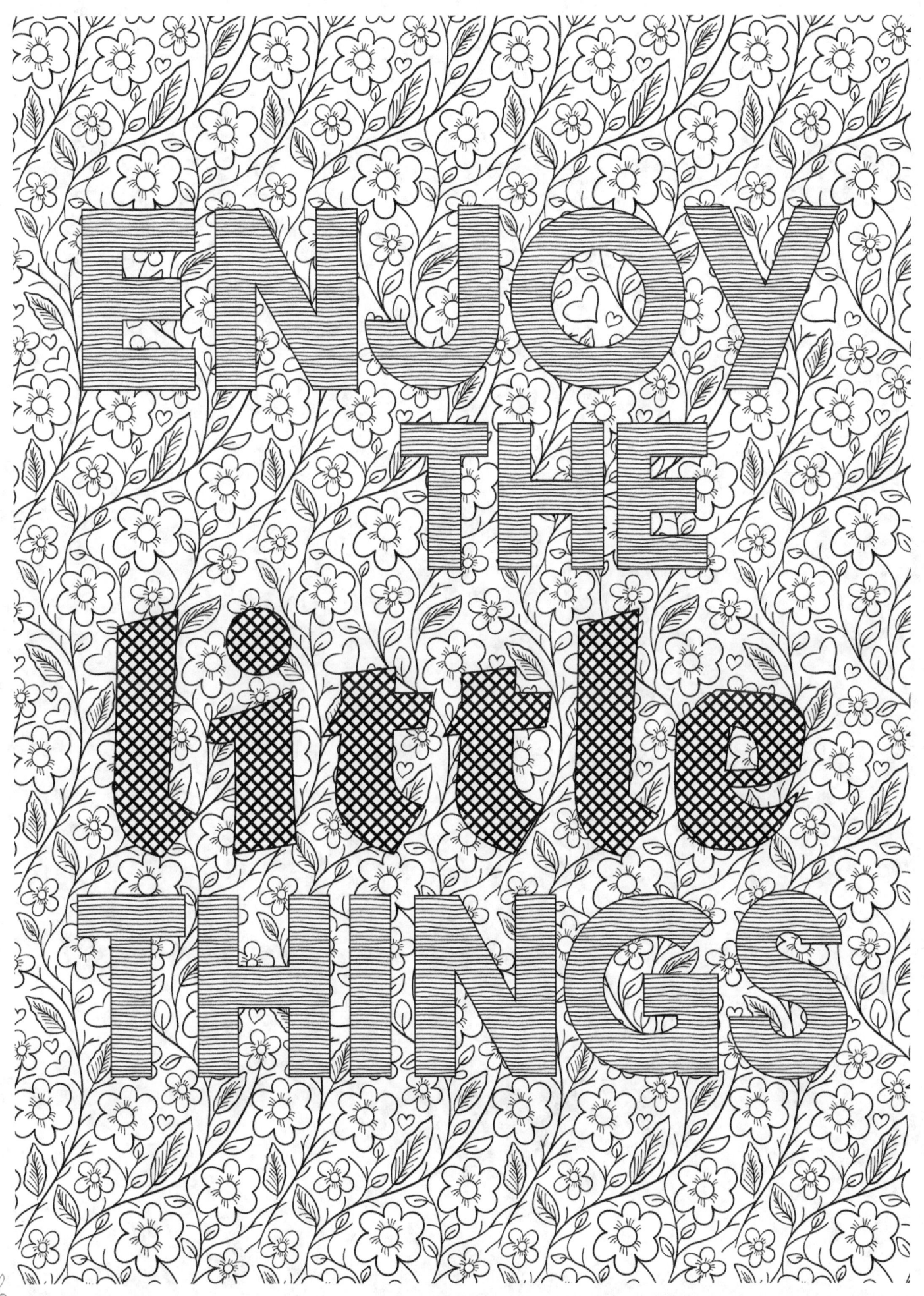

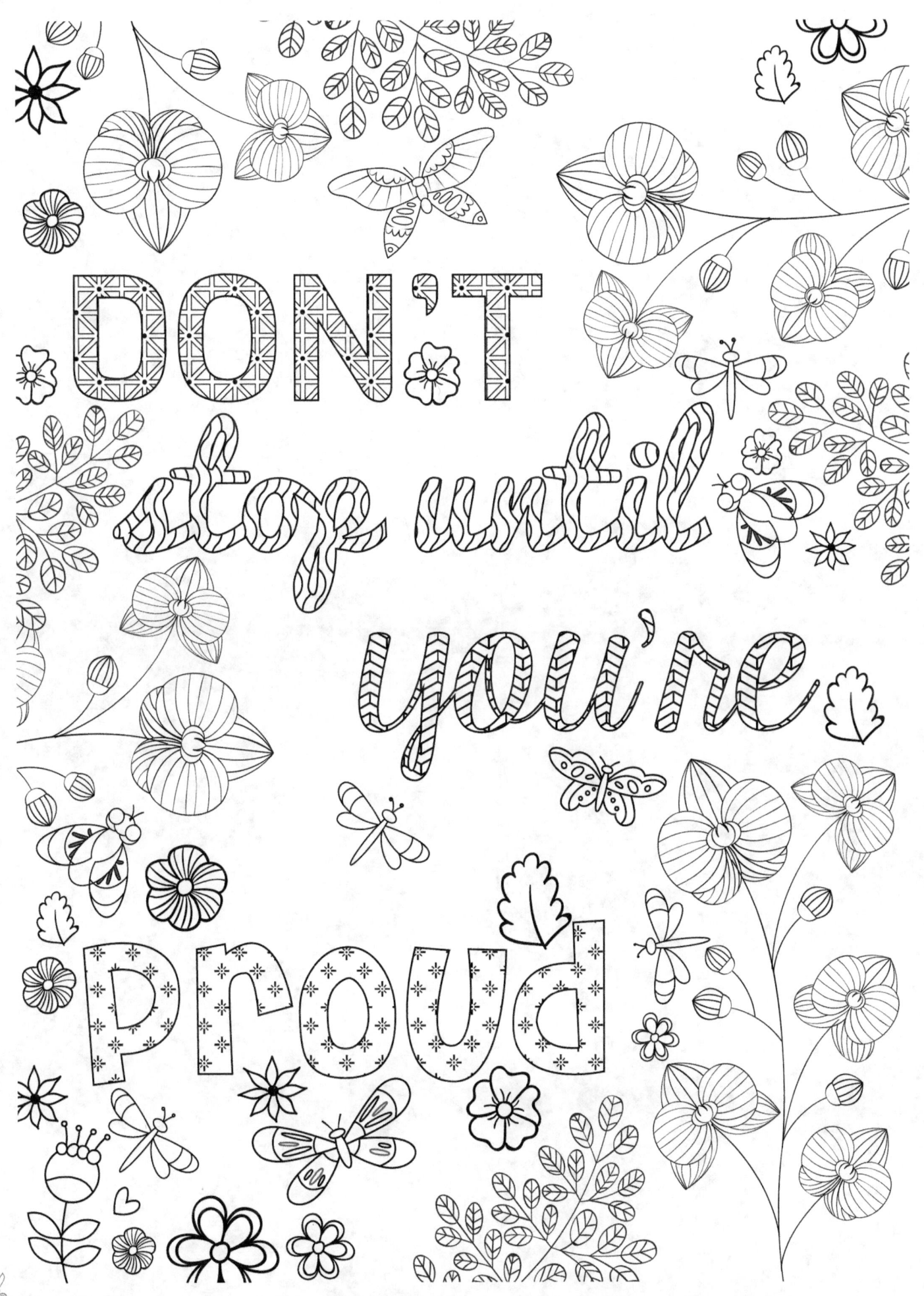

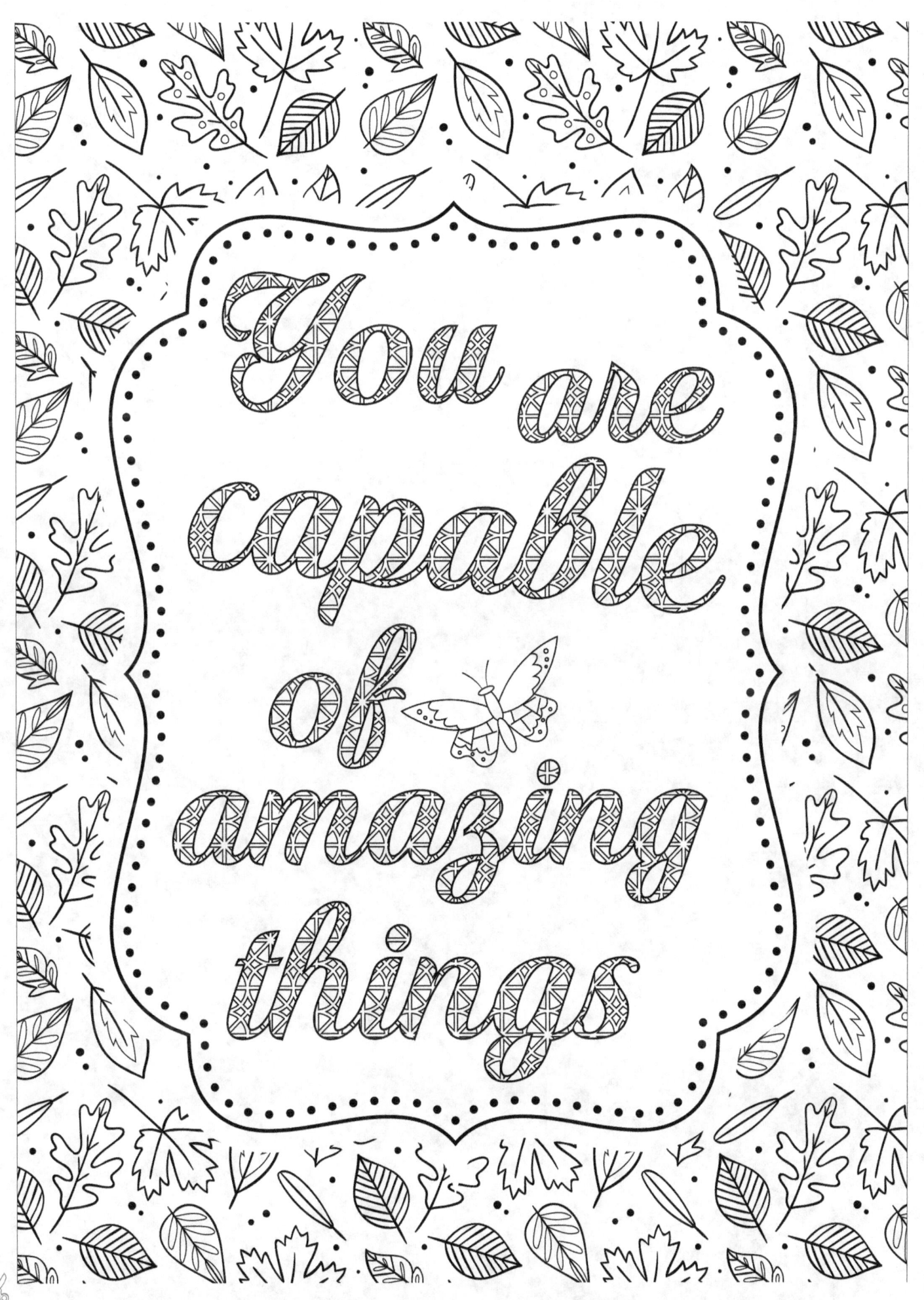

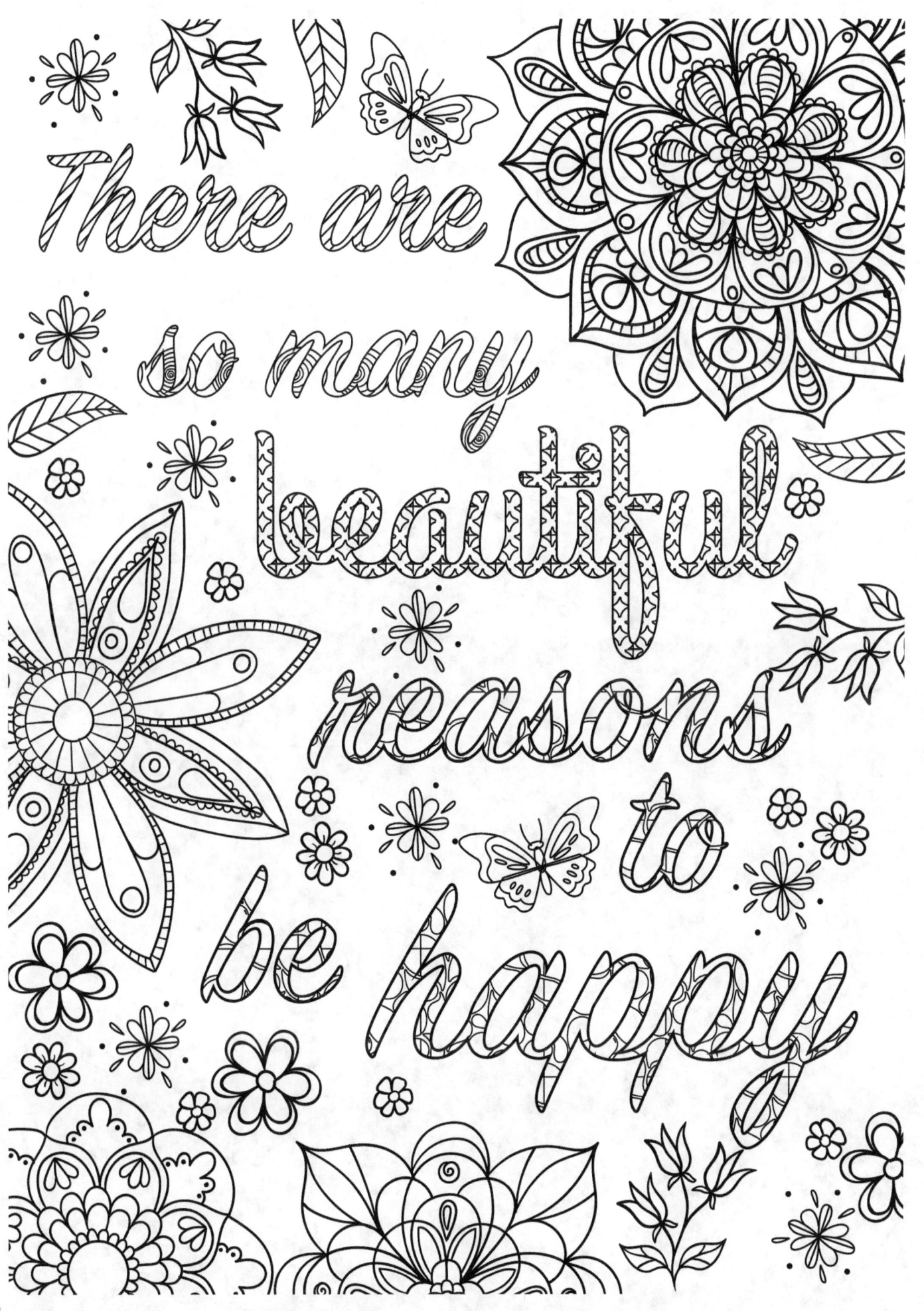

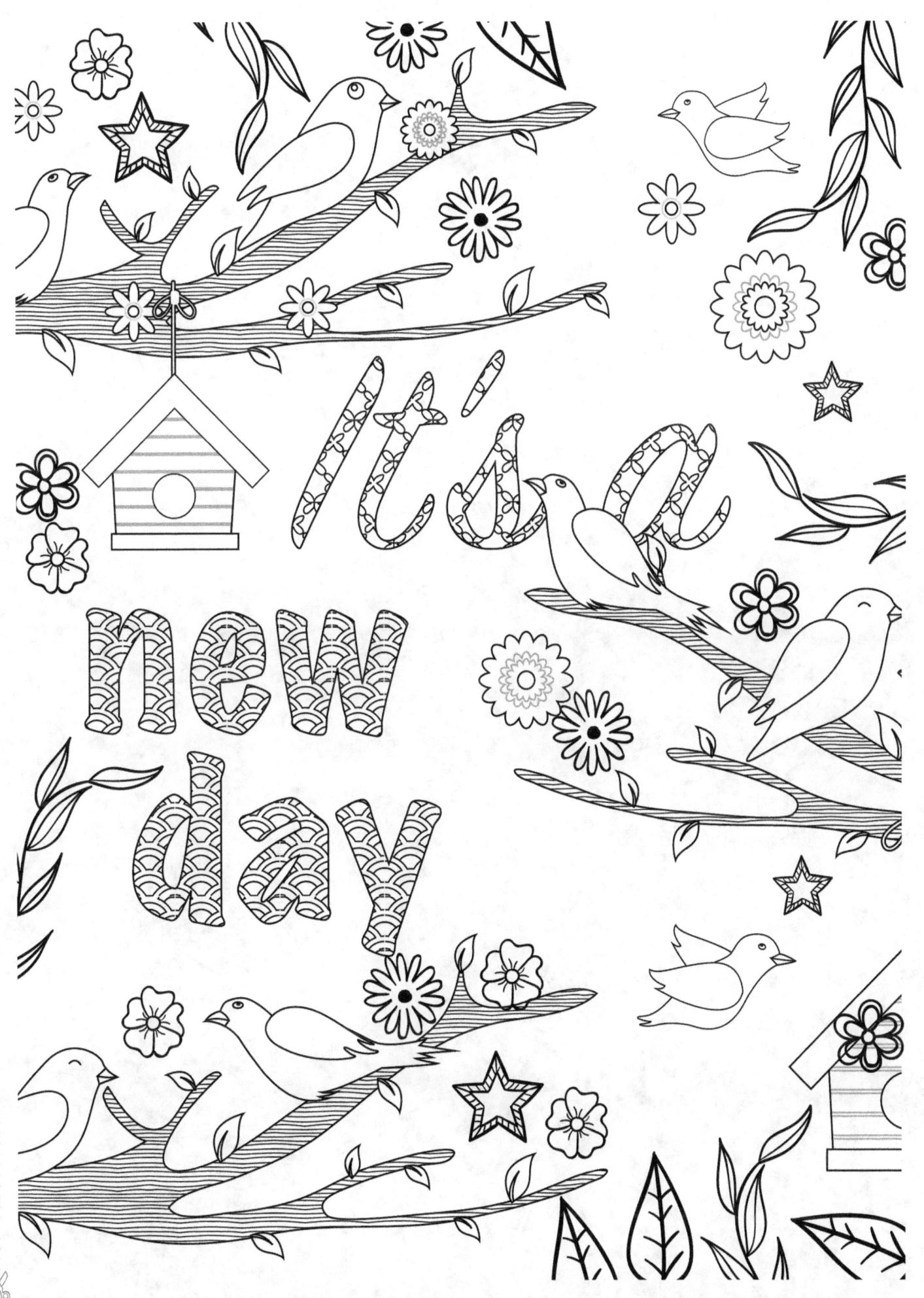

It's a new day

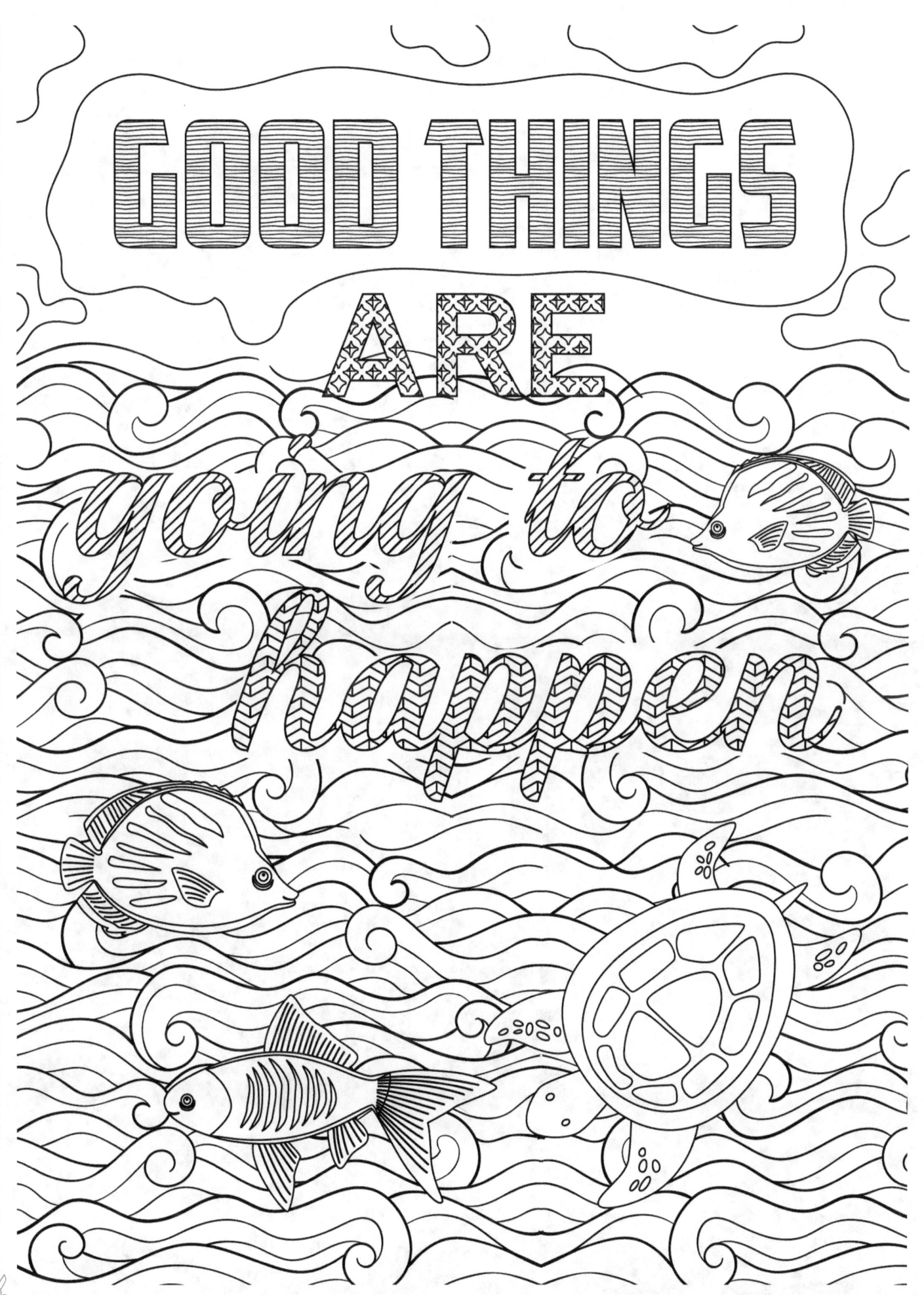

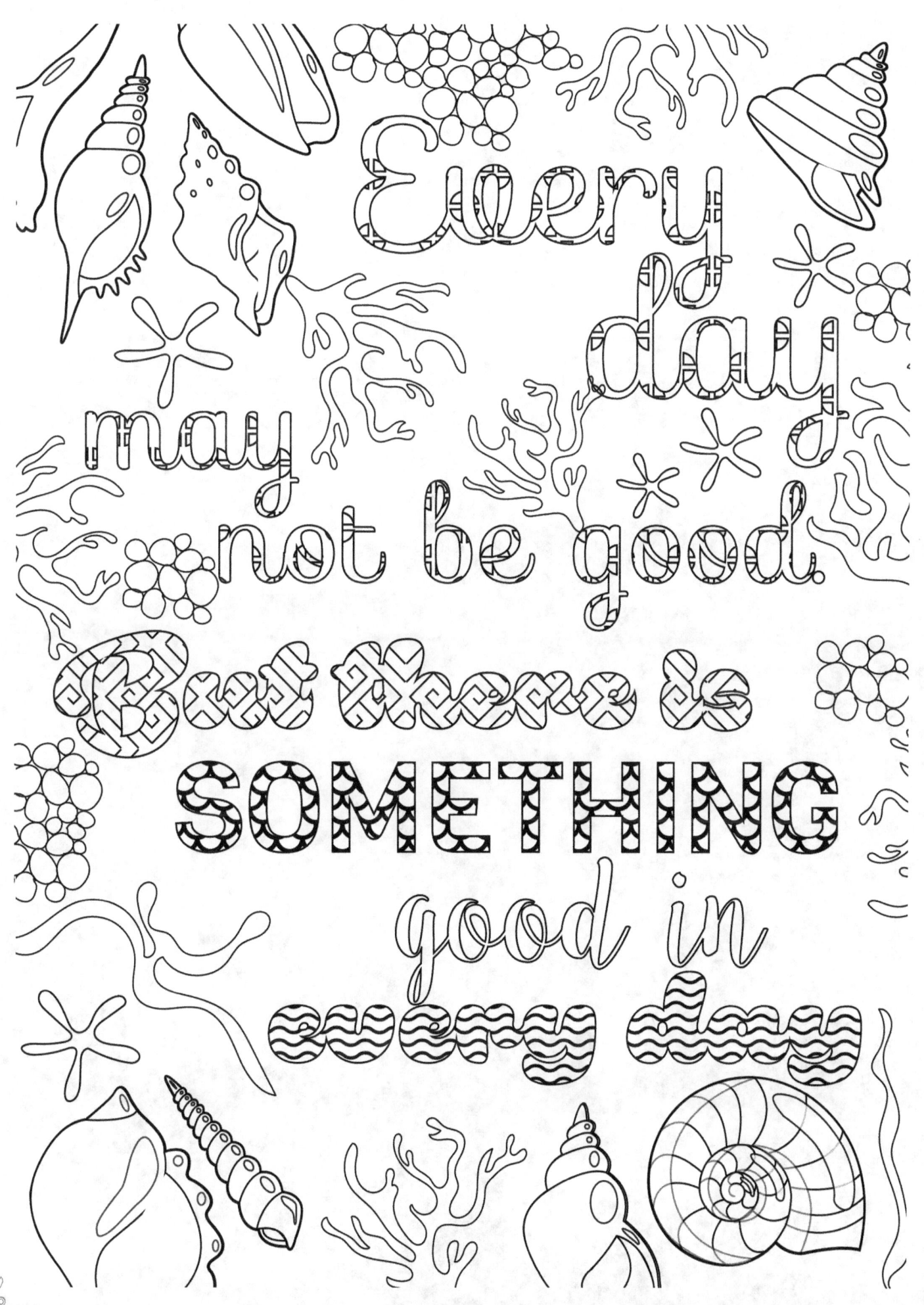

Every day may not be good. But there is SOMETHING good in every day

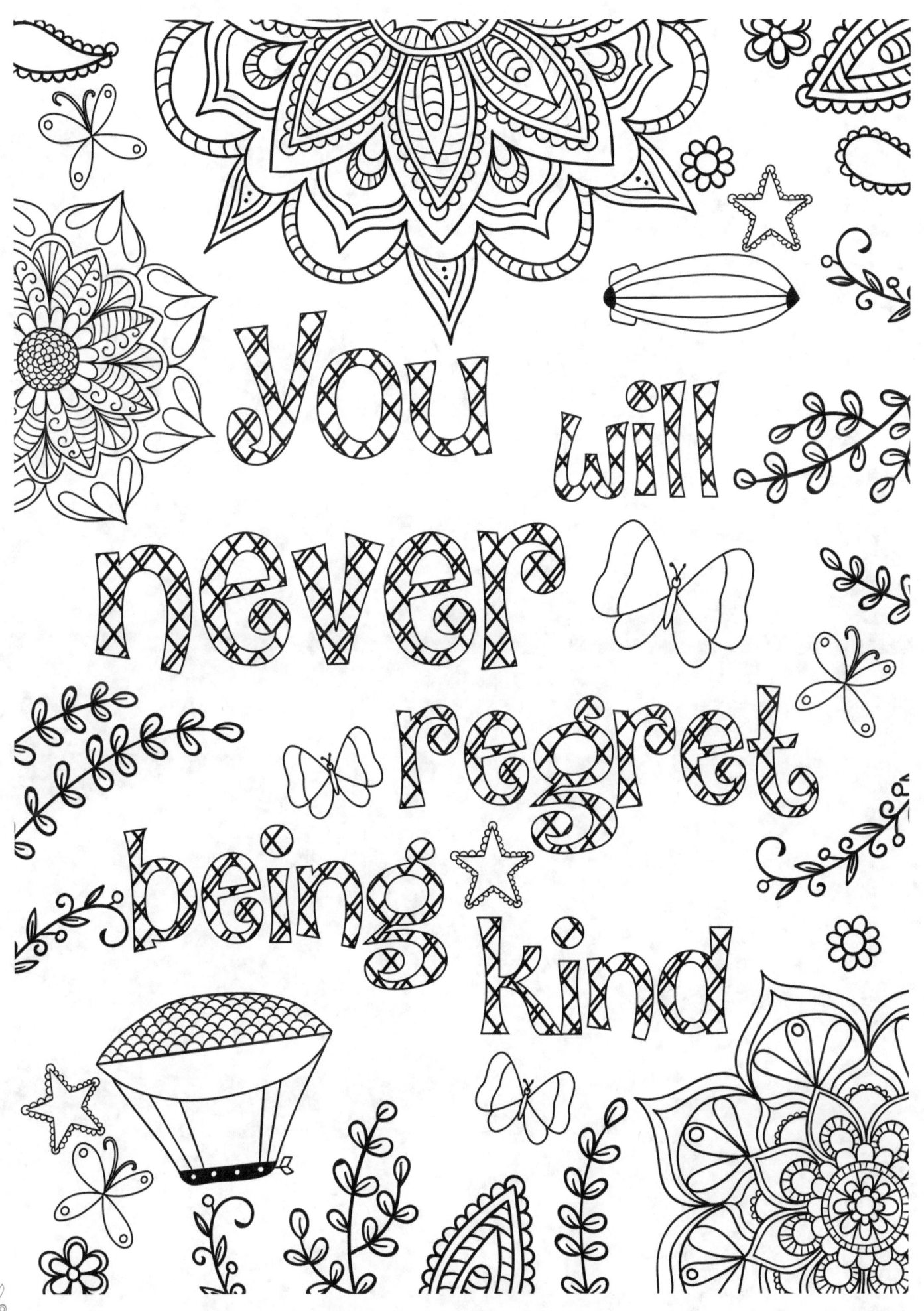

You will never regret being kind

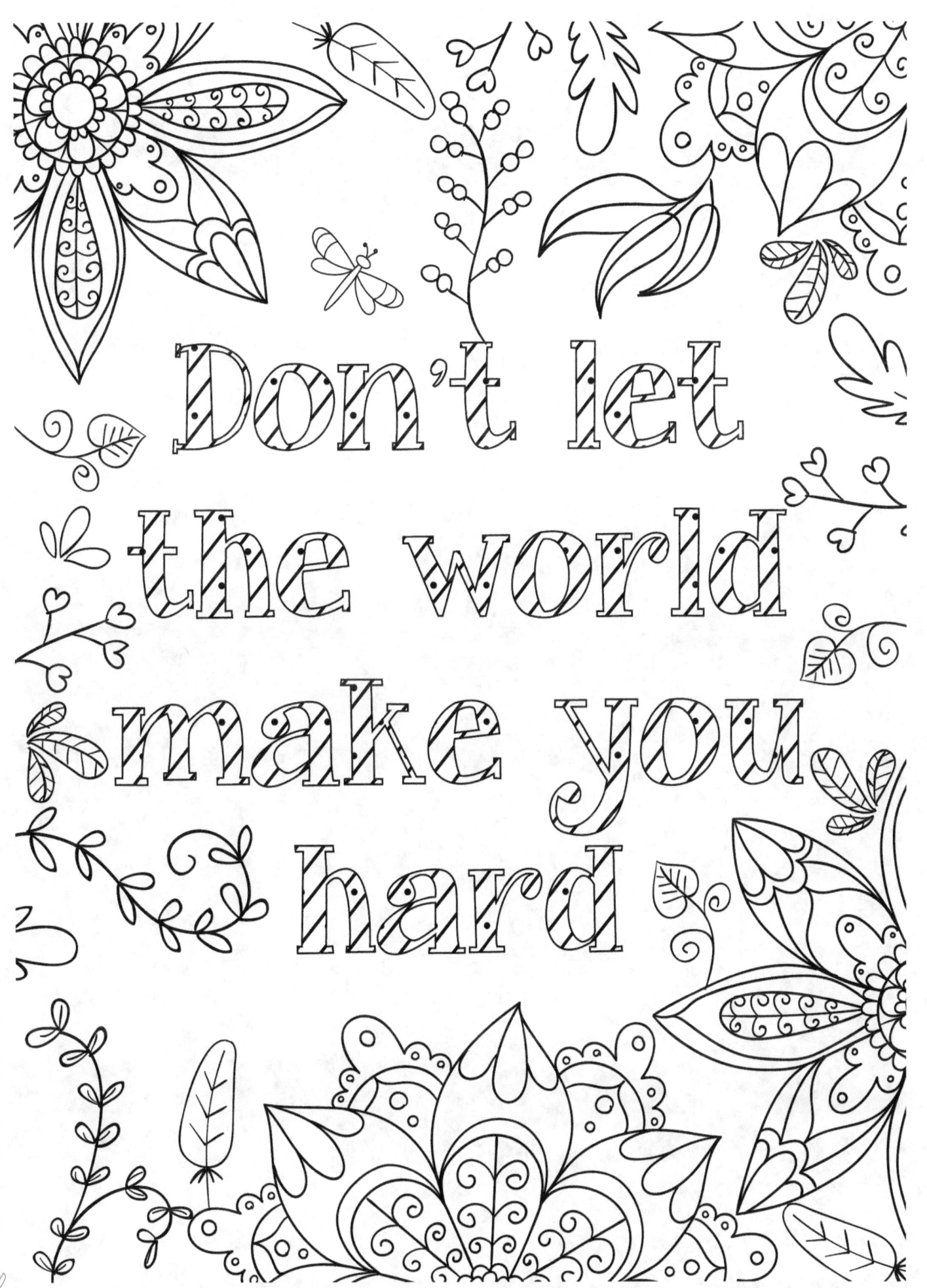

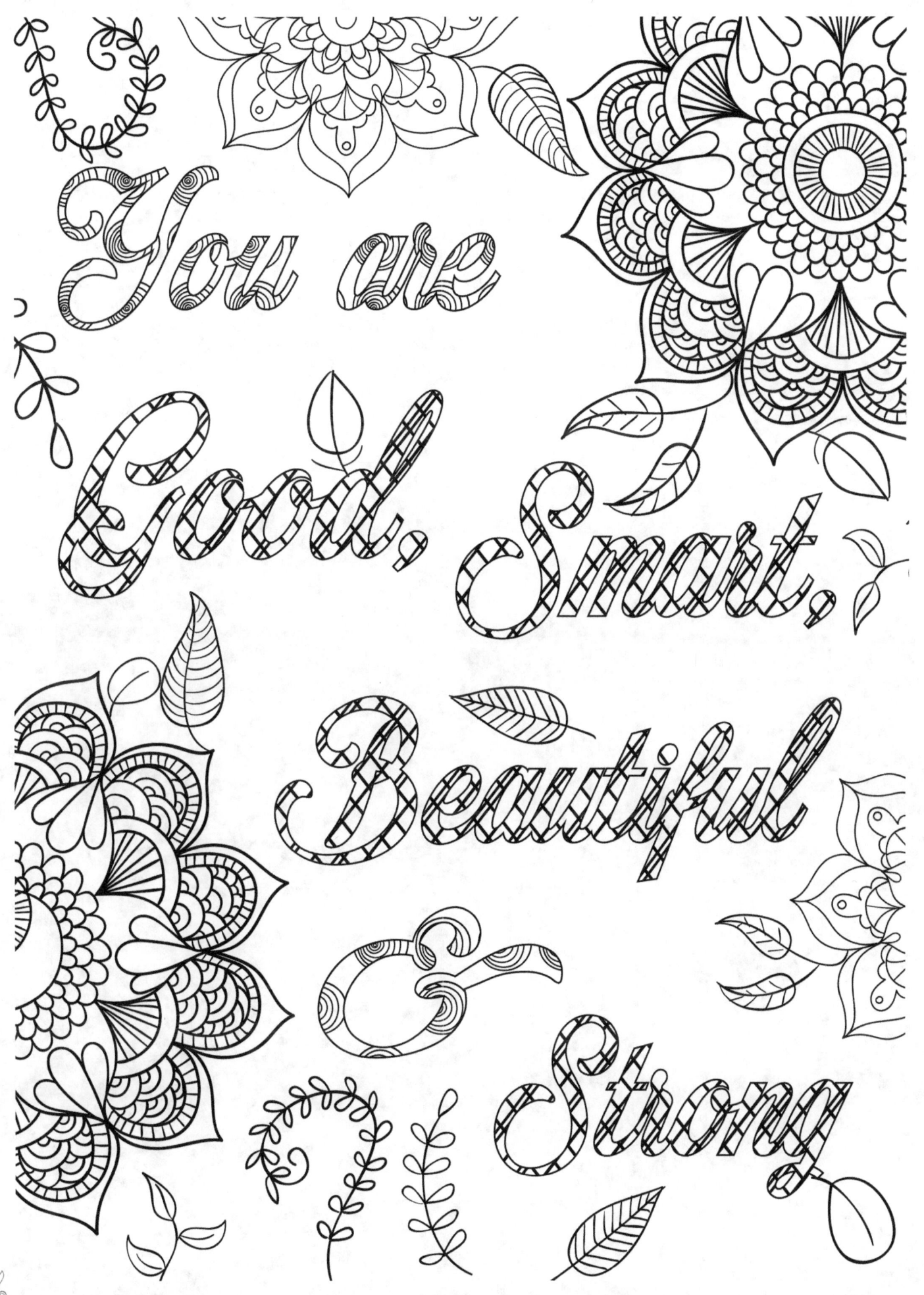

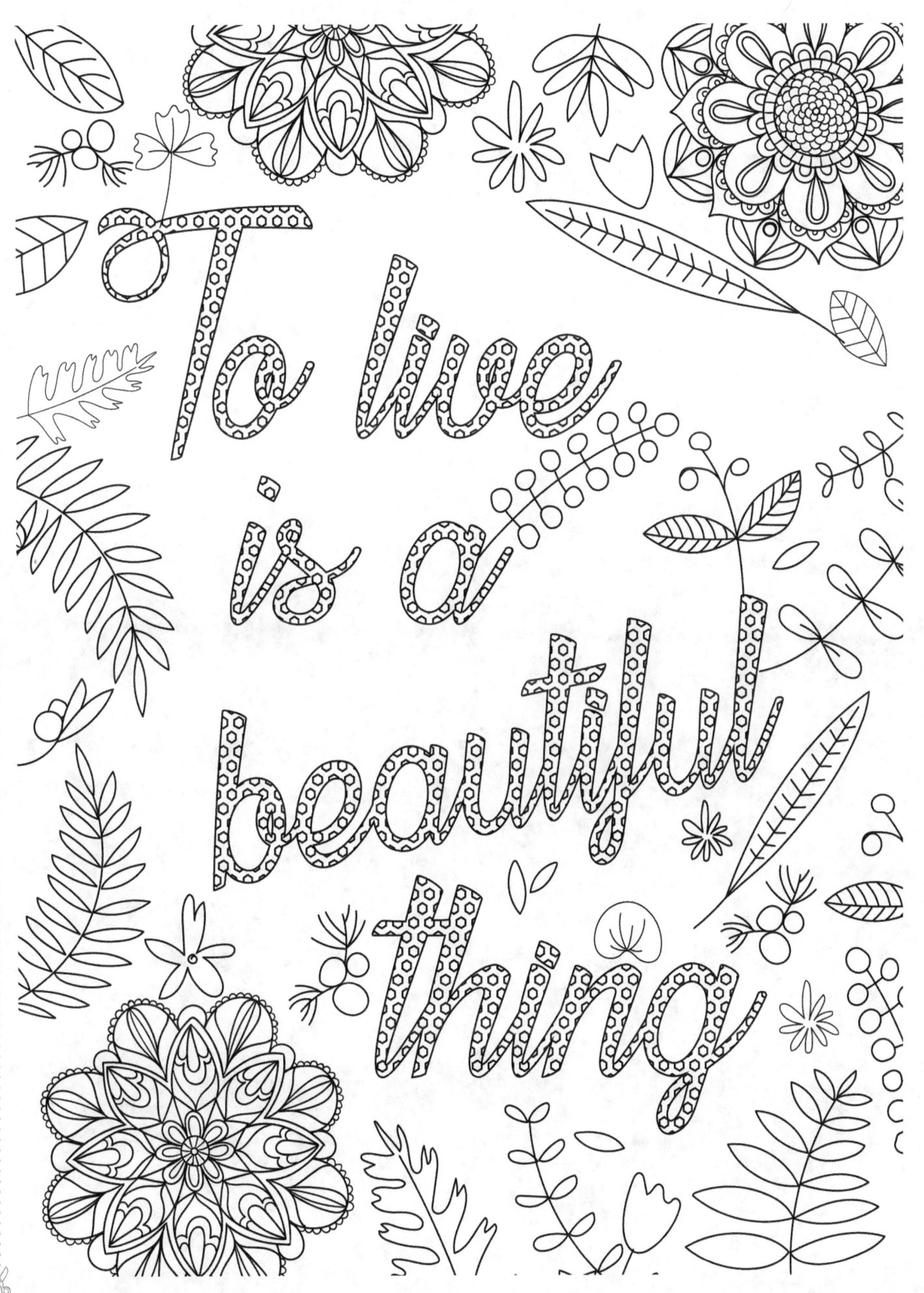

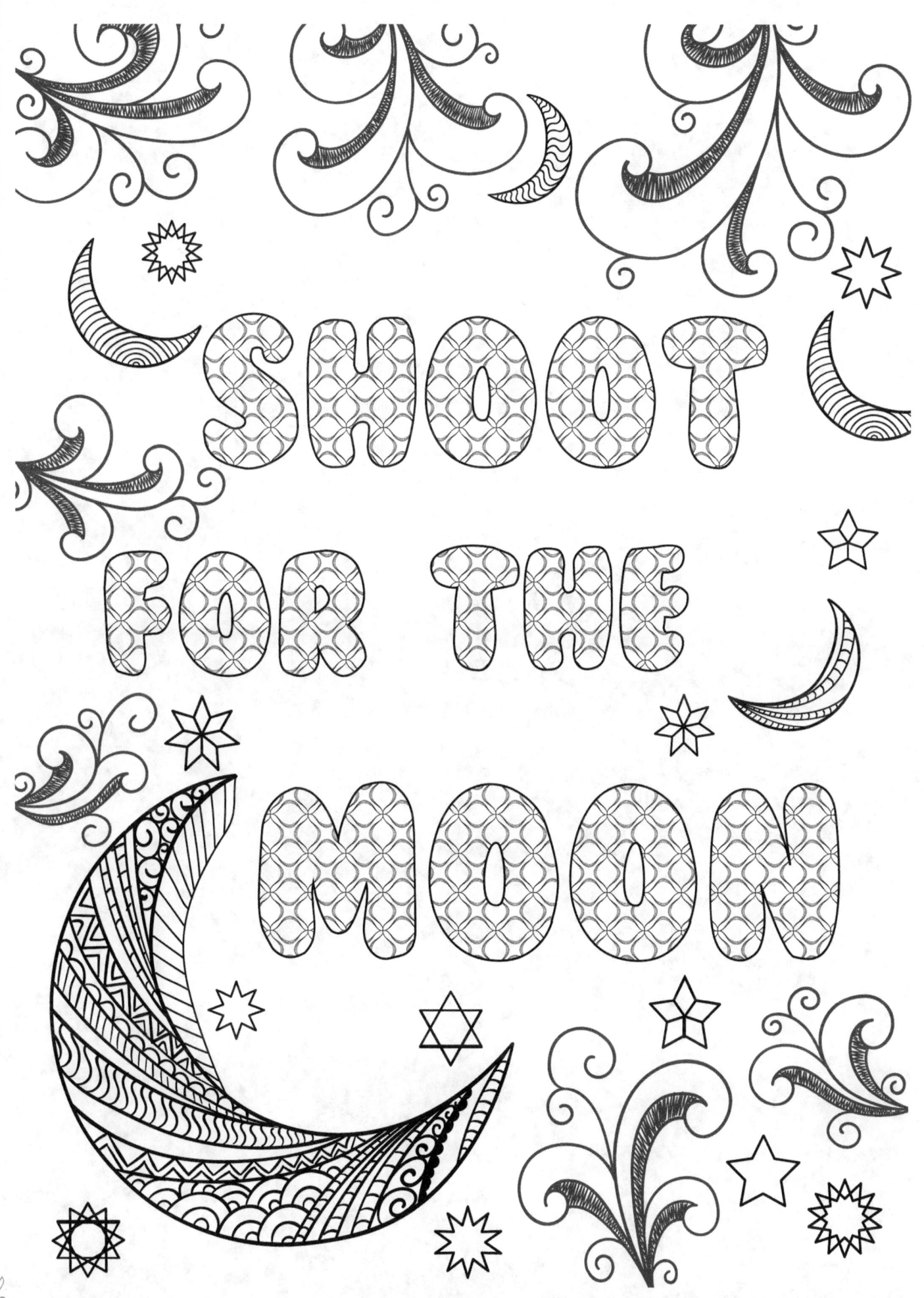

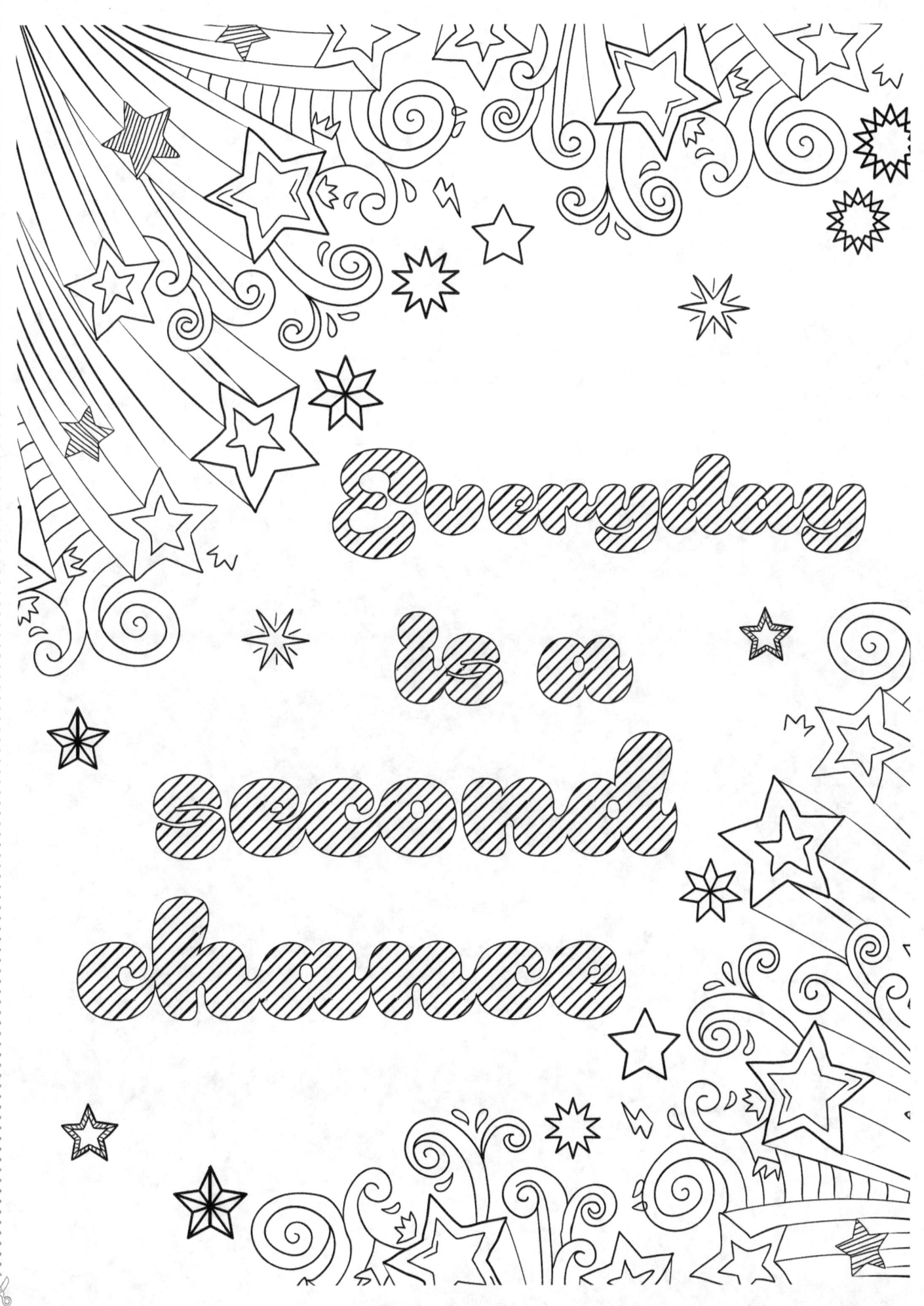

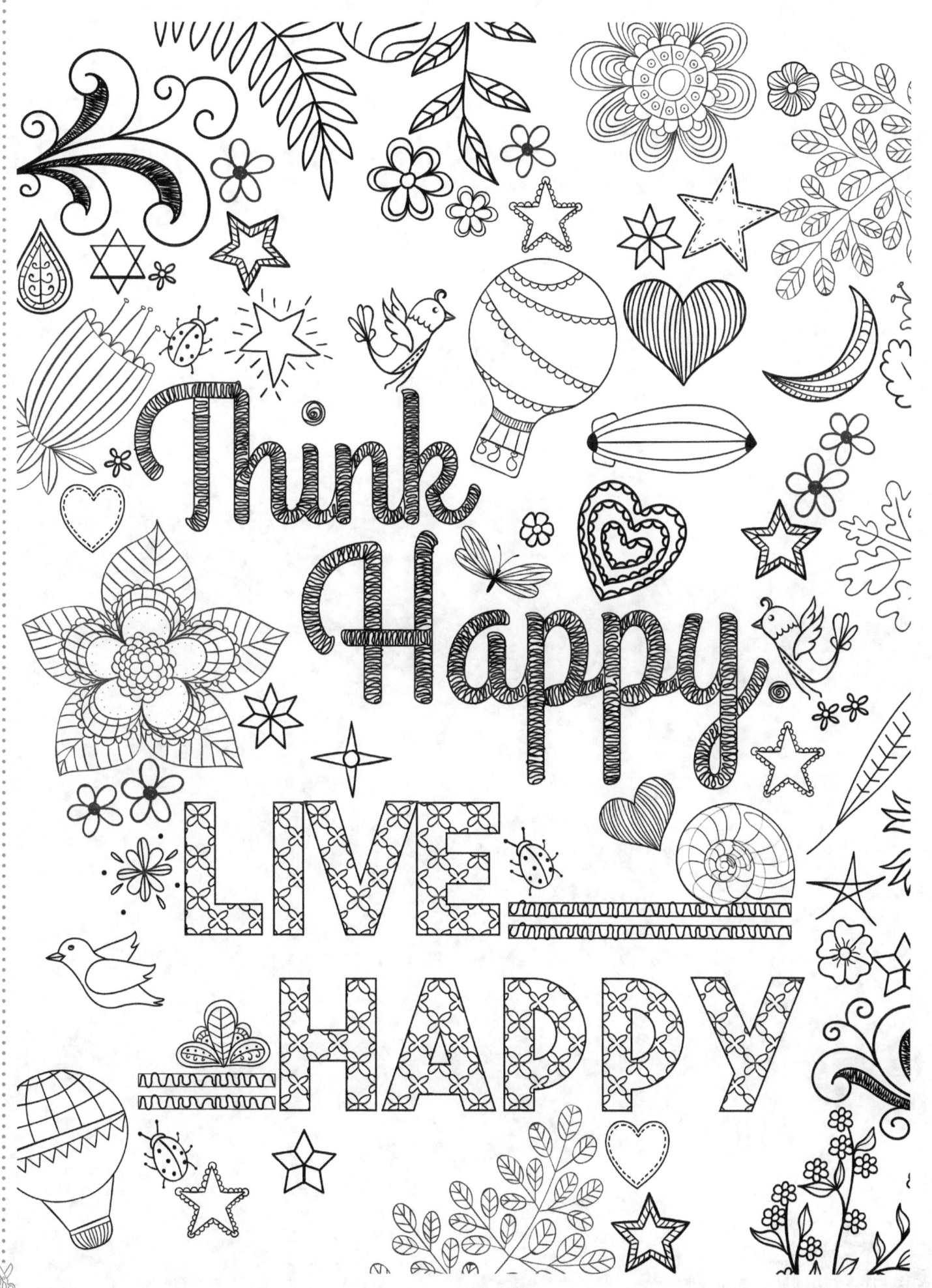